W9-DGB-332
DISCARDED

920.02
B72s

81411

DATE DUE			

SAINTS AND SINNERS

THOMAS À KEMPIS

SAINTS and SINNERS

BY GAMALIEL BRADFORD

WITH ILLUSTRATIONS

KENNIKAT PRESS
Port Washington, N. Y./London

CARL A. RUDISILL LIBRARY
LENOIR RHYNE COLLEGE

920.02
B72s
81411
Jan. 1973

SAINTS AND SINNERS

Copyright, 1931, by the Missionary Society of St. Paul
The Apostle in The State of New York
Copyright, 1931 and 1932, by Duke University Press
Copyright, 1932, by Gamaliel Bradford
Reissued in 1971 by Kennikat Press by arrangement
with Houghton Mifflin Co.
Library of Congress Catalog Card No: 74-118459
ISBN 0-8046-1401-6

Manufactured by Taylor Publishing Company   Dallas, Texas

ESSAY AND GENERAL LITERATURE INDEX REPRINT SERIES

TO
OLIVER ORR
DEVOTED SUPPORTER AND LOYAL FRIEND

'"Fool!" said my Muse to me, "look in thy heart and write."'

SIR PHILIP SIDNEY

CONTENTS

ILLUSTRATIONS

SAINTS AND SINNERS

I

THE RIOT OF YOUTH
CÆSAR BORGIA

CHRONOLOGY

CESARE BORGIA, DUKE OF VALENTINOIS, etc.
Born, Rome, 1475(?).
At University of Perugia, 1488.
Father became Pope as Alexander VI, 1492.
Cardinal, 1493.
Resigned Cardinalate, 1498.
Married Charlotte d'Albret, 1499.
Became Duke of Romagna, 1501.
Triumphed over rebel condottieri at Sinigaglia,
    December 31, 1502.
Alexander VI died, August 18, 1503.
Sent to Spain, August, 1504.
Escaped from Spanish prison, October, 1506.
Killed at Viana, March 12, 1507.

CESARE BORGIA
From the Portrait by Giorgione

SAINTS AND SINNERS

I

THE RIOT OF YOUTH
CÆSAR BORGIA

I

AN AGE that had shaken off the shackles and trammels of superstition, had rid itself of the meaningless taboos of a priest-ridden and fear-ridden past and let its will and its intelligence go free, unencumbered by any restraints save those of expediency and sanity and common sense, an age in which the men were strong and purposeful and self-reliant and the women allowed themselves to do anything and say anything and think anything and wear anything — or nothing — secure that their prominence and dominance would be firmer than ever, an age that rioted in the comfort and abundance and beauty of material things, feeling that after the darkness of the Puritanic years it had a royal right to revel and enjoy — am I speaking of twentieth-century America or of the Italy of the Renaissance?

Cæsar Borgia was the true child of his age: he felt that he was born into a world of luxuriant splendor, with keen senses and superlative powers, and from his youth to his early death he used the senses and the powers to engross and make his own every morsel of splendor that he possibly could. Cæsar was born in 1475, or thereabouts, the son of a great church dignitary, Rodrigo Borgia, who later bought the Papacy, as others bought it before and after him. From his childhood Cæsar was destined for the Church and was loaded with lucrative and dignified preferments up to the cardinalate. He was well educated and trained for every intellectual and practical achievement, and when his father became Pope Alexander the Sixth, in 1492, his great object in life was to exalt and establish Cæsar and his other children as permanent ecclesiastical and temporal dignitaries. When Cæsar's younger brother, the Duke of Gandia, was murdered in 1497, by Cæsar's agency as was popularly supposed, he grew restless with religion, threw it off, and set himself to carve a military and political dominion in central Italy out of the States of the Church. He endeavored to accomplish this by marriage with the royal house of France and by crushing the petty sovereigns who tyrannized throughout the Romagna, and he seemed in a fair way to magnificent success when his dream edifice was shattered by the sudden death of the Pope in 1503. Cæsar's desperate illness at the same time prevented his controlling the situation. His bitter enemy became Pope as Julius II. And Julius, after trifling with Cæsar for a while, handed him over to the hostility of Spain, in which country he was imprisoned for two years. He managed with the ut-

4

most daring and peril to escape, and fled to France, where he was killed in 1507, when he was just over thirty. In thinking of him, his youth, his mere boyishness, must never be forgotten any more than with Alexander, or with Keats or Chatterton. He was at the top of the world before he was twenty, and into the next ten years he crowded the passion, the aspiration, the turbulence, the tragedy, and the wickedness, of a long, long life.

In dealing with Cæsar Borgia, we have to face at once the difficulty of getting into his soul, and as in all such cases the difficulty adds immensely to the charm. It is not only that he lived four hundred years ago and is therefore obscured by the haze of accumulated centuries. He himself cultivated mystery and loved it, both because it helped his dark and tortuous dealings, and because it seemed to foster the remote, unique grandeur which he sought and loved. Always there is a flavor of Elizabethan tragedy about him, of the heroes of Shakespeare or Webster or Marston, the lurid suggestion of deliberate wickedness, with just a touch of the ever-present theatrical. That acute and profound observer, Machiavelli, who was close to Cæsar in the most critical moments and tried hard to gauge him, murmurs in despair: 'No one knows what course he is going to take, for it is difficult to penetrate his designs and to know him.' Assuredly it is no easier today than four hundred years ago.

We can at least begin to approach Cæsar most

safely from the external aspect, from his superb natural health and his magnificent physique, which went far in the accomplishment of his objects. We have no very satisfactorily reliable likenesses of him, but we know that in his youth at any rate he was impressive and delightful to look at, charming men and women both. We know still more surely that he had unusual and even phenomenal muscular strength. He could bear the fatigue of long, sudden marches and extreme exposure to heat and cold which prostrated the most enduring. He could break stout poles and strong cords with his hands and could wrench a horseshoe into any shape he wished. He rejoiced in hardy outdoor sports and always took a prominent and successful part in them. He used to make his young officers go out and challenge the rustics to contests of skill and strength and he recognized excellence in these things and rewarded it wherever he met with it. He was instrumental in importing the bull-fight from his Spanish fatherland to Rome, believing that it was less likely to cripple permanently than the tournament. And he rejoiced in exhibiting his own prowess against the bulls in the arena. On one occasion he joined a group of matadors in attacking two loose bulls and himself attacked the more ferocious one of them single-handed. At another time, as the old chronicler tells us, he assailed a bull and 'cut off his head at one stroke, a thing which to all Rome appeared most extraordinary.' As Anatole France puts it, happily, 'It is probable that in his eager life

6

the greatest delight he ever knew was that of using the inexhaustible power of his muscles.'

But the mere play of the muscles was by no means the whole of Cæsar Borgia. From a very early period he cherished long designs of distinction and glory and sought steadily to build himself a great temporal dominion with all the power of the Papacy behind him — 'a vast soul and one that seeks greatness and fame,' as was said by an observer who had watched him closely. To this end he studied every means of connection and alliance and penetrated with the shrewdest intelligence into the complicated network of intrigue and scheming ambition which covered the whole of Italy at that time. His extraordinary quickness and acuteness in these matters, even as a boy in the twenties, was what drew the respect and admiration of the attentive and discriminating Machiavelli.

What is curious and notable in Cæsar's political progress is the blending of a habit of wise and just administration with the most subtle and unscrupulous cunning proceeding even to treachery, the latter being pushed to such a point that one is apt to attribute the former rather to far-reaching policy than to sympathetic human kindliness. The duplicity attained its climax in the device which outwitted and destroyed a group of rebellious subordinates at Sinigaglia, a device incredibly base and crooked in itself, yet one which gained almost universal admiration among contemporaries as much by its cleverness and success as by the un-

deniable fact that the victims of it richly deserved
all they got. As to this matter of duplicity, however, nothing can be more instructive than the
comments of Machiavelli, even while he admires.
'If one could believe him to be sincere,' he remarks
on one occasion, 'we might rest assured without
any uneasiness. But the experience of others
makes one fear for one's self.' And another touch
is still more illuminating: 'The Duke meantime
allows himself to be carried away by his sanguine
confidence, believing that the word of others is
more to be relied upon than his own.'

The excellence of Cæsar's administration in the
provinces that he had made his own is more agree-
able to dwell upon and is attested by even his
enemies. He established a rule that was just in
theory, and he was zealous, attentive, and persistent in seeing that the rule was evenly and
honestly applied, so that everywhere he made himself popular, at any rate in contrast to the petty
tyrants who had preceded him. And though his
remark that he came not to tyrannize but to destroy tyrants is one usual enough with conquerors,
it seems to have as much justice as it had with
Napoleon.

By means of the justice — and the duplicity —
Cæsar appeared to be triumphantly accomplishing
his ends. Then with the Pope's death came downfall and utter tragedy. The interesting thing here
as always is the psychological change. From a
secure exaltation that seemed unshakable by any

chance the man's mood shifted to doubt, discouragement, despair. 'The blows of fortune, which he is not accustomed to bear, have stunned and confounded him,' says the ever watchful Machiavelli. The most notable incident in this connection is the scene in which Cæsar humbles himself before Guidobaldo of Montefeltro, whom in happier days he had hunted from his throne and dominion. 'We are told by an eye-witness that Valentinois entered cap in hand and twice bent his knees to the ground in advancing towards Duke Guidobaldo....[He] humbly besought forgiveness for the past....He promised to restore all the stolen property....He continued to bear himself towards all with the same abject servility.' All which must have been a torturing discipline for that haughty, unbroken spirit — unless, unless we may assume a profound dissimulation beneath it.

But all this was far, far away and quite unimagined in the earlier days of triumph, when Machiavelli wrote of 'the Duke with his unheard-of good fortune, with a courage and confidence almost superhuman, and believing himself capable of accomplishing whatever he undertakes.' In those sunshiny days of glory and success, when everything seemed to be coming his way, there was no thought of doffing caps or bowing knees, but only of being bowed down to and fawned upon. Every agency of power and achievement seemed to be ready to his hand. Money? Was there not a doting father, with all the vast resources of the

Church, eager to pour them out as they were wanted and even more? If cash was called for, all you had to do was to make a batch of cardinals and let them pay. And Cæsar was magnificent in his generosity and wildly sumptuous in his expenditure, till even the doting father grumbled a little: 'He is royal, even prodigal, and this displeases the Pope.'

And as there was ample money, so there was ample fighting power, which was even more requisite. It is not necessary to assume, as some do, that Cæsar was one of the great incipient generals of the world. There have been a good many of them. But surely he was more than the spoiled impetuous boy that others consider him. He was one of the first to use a conscripted militia instead of relying altogether upon mercenaries, and that he could do this and still retain his popularity is surely some evidence of power. He was quick and shrewd in his vision of what ought to be done in a military way and swiftly decided as well as uncompromisingly firm in doing it. Here again the judgment of the enthusiastic but clear-sighted Machiavelli is hard to resist: 'When it is a question of winning glory and enlarging his territories, he knows neither repose, nor fatigue, nor danger; you hardly hear of his arrival in a place before he is away again; he knows how to make the soldiers love him; he has got together the best troops in Italy; and all these circumstances, joined to an extraordinary good fortune, make him a victor to be feared.'

So in these days of triumph and splendor the

sense of spontaneous, vivid, inexhaustible vitality is overwhelming. 'Nothing is more remarkable than the fulness of the life that throbbed in them,' says Symonds of Cæsar and his contemporaries. It is certainly true of Cæsar himself. It was the life, the vigor, the abounding energy of youth let loose, with all the gorgeousness of this world before it. The days and the nights were one continuous revel. Sometimes there was a touch of the fantastic and extravagant about it, as the Venetian ambassador remarks, 'his fantasies are simply unintelligible,' doubtless referring to such freaks as the boyish Carnival trick of wandering masked with a group of friends through the streets of Cesena, picking up mud and spattering it over every passer-by. But the freaks are more winning when they have beauty and imagination in them, as in the account of the joyous merry-making in Pesaro when news of the marriage of Cæsar's sister was received there: 'They danced in the great hall, and the couples, hand in hand, issued from the castle, led by Monsignor Scaltes, the Pope's plenipotentiary; the people in their joy joined in and danced away the hours in the streets of the city.' Which surely was daffing the time carelessly, as they did in the golden world.

II

This free, joyous, intoxicated revel in the life of the immediate present is the supreme characteristic of the Renaissance, the rebirth, the rediscovery of this human world in which we live, and such is the deeper significance of the name. Renaissance is often assumed to be identical with Revival of Learning, and the fall of the Eastern Empire with the taking of Constantinople by the Turks and the consequent dissemination of the remains of Greek culture throughout Western Europe are supposed to be responsible for the initiation of the modern spirit. But the Middle Ages are now known to have been more permeated with classical learning than was formerly imagined and the spirit of the Renaissance was far more than a mere intellectual resuscitation. With the reëstablishment of comparative peace and order and urban living, after the political chaos of the Middle Ages, men began to feel the charm, the inexhaustible, varied riches of the delights and diversions of this world, and for the time it seemed as if this world was almost enough, at any rate enough to keep the shadowy, ghostly, mediæval other world largely forgotten and obscured.

But what is chiefly notable about the Renaissance is that its enjoyment of the revel of the senses, its keen appreciation of the glory and the splendor of material things, is deeply transfigured by imaginative beauty. Men were not content with the mere ecstasy of momentary sensation, they always sought to heighten and enrich and immortalize it by the addition of ideal charm, and painting and sculpture and architecture and poetry gave an eternal significance which the mere revel of the senses could never hope to attain. In Italy, the Italy of the Borgias, this imaginative outburst reached its highest perfection in painting, and the names of Botticelli, of Perugino, of Raphael, of Michael Angelo, of the Venetians, still represent the climax of all that the brush has ever done. In poetry Ariosto and Tasso are great names, but they are pale beside Dante. The truth is that painting alone in Italy escaped being influenced and to some extent obscured by the classical tradition. Sculpture, architecture, even literature, were hampered and restrained by Greek and Latin models and could not work out their destiny with untrammeled freedom. You have to pass over into Spain and into England to find the Renaissance joy of this world in its highest national literary expression and the drama of Shakespeare and his fellows is perhaps an even more perfect interpretation of the Renaissance spirit than is the painting of Italy.

What concerns us is, of course, the relation of Cæsar Borgia to the Renaissance and the Renaissance spirit of beauty. In that age the artist lived mainly by patronage; not the patronage of the great public, but the patronage of the restricted few who had the money and who had the power. Men like the Medicis, especially the great Pope Leo X, with other sovereigns of similar tastes, entered thoroughly into the artistic movement about them, and not only encouraged great painters and architects but understood them. There seems to be no evidence that the Borgias were of this type.

Pope Alexander had himself painted by Pinturic-
chio, took some interest in building, and did whatever he did lavishly. But his tastes were for more
concrete pleasures than those of the imagination.
The same appears to be true of Cæsar. He had
some contact with Michael Angelo and Pinturic-
chio. He attached Leonardo to himself, but it was
more to use him as a military engineer than as a
painter. Cæsar gathered poets about him — to
sing his praises. He is even said to have given them
a suggestion or two occasionally. But he had no
such delight in literary activity as had Lorenzo de'
Medici.

Again, as the Renaissance transfigured the life of
this material world by imaginative beauty, so it
also transformed and elevated that life by intellectual effort. Everywhere there was an immense,
restless, perturbed movement of thought, striving
in the blind endeavor to shift from the authorita-
tive attitude of the Middle Ages to the free spiritual
probing and soaring of the Modern World. This
was felt in scholarship, it was felt in philosophy, it
was felt above all in science, and the vast intellectual exploration of Copernicus and Galileo led
straight up to modern experimental research and
practically to the discovery of America. Once more
one looks for the Borgias in all this. Apparently the
chief intellectual achievement of Alexander was the
invention of the censorship. With the discovery
of printing and the consequent rapid spread of
books, there was an obvious tendency, especially

with the other moral elements of the time, to a wide and dissipating disorder, and it may be that a certain amount of checking was essential. Still, it will never add greatly to a sovereign's intellectual reputation that he was the first to apply a system which has done more than any other one thing to hamper and harass and impede intellectual progress.

Nor is there much more to be said for Cæsar in this connection. His own intelligence was quick, acute, and penetrating enough; few were more so. Those who had occasion to discuss with him were immensely impressed with his powers of response and retort, '*dello ingegno et della lingua si vale quanto vuole* — he avails himself of wit and words just as he pleases.' But there is no reason to suppose that he cared to apply these gifts to abstract ratiocination. He had ample use for them in getting wealth and pleasure for Cæsar Borgia: why should he look beyond these?

The one form in which the Renaissance imagination and love of beauty appears in Cæsar is the concrete, material aspect of the taste for ornament and splendor. He loved to dignify himself and those about him with all the decoration that wealth and artistic ingenuity could afford. When he went to France to be married, his train was equipped with a dazzling gorgeousness that disgusted Brantôme, who exclaimed against 'the vain glory and extravagant pretence of this Duke Valentino.' It was even said that he shod his horses with precious metal, expecting that the shoes would fall off and be gathered up by the poor. A rich, splendidly colored garment, a magnificently ornamented weapon, these were things that appealed to him always. It was partly the eternal youth in him, reveling in color and display. It was even more that such things were most powerful agencies for working on the imaginations of men and women, and to subdue men and women, to mould them to his will, and to make his kingdom, his glory, and his pleasure out of them, was to him the supreme object of existence.

III

As to Cæsar's dealing with women, the history of it is even more obscure, mythical, and perplexing than the other aspects of his career. To understand these dealings we must first establish some notion as to the general condition of sexual morals and this is as difficult as it always is. To infer that condition from the gay and licentious stories of Boccaccio's *Decameron* and other novelists of the day would be as unreasonable as to judge the sexual morals of present-day America by the novels that pour from the presses of New York. In the Italy of Vittoria Colonna there were undoubtedly thousands and thousands of noble women leading quiet, pure, God-fearing, domestic lives, just as there are millions of such women in America today. Also, even in the *Decameron* itself there is at least a veneer of refined courtesy and gracious consideration which

would not seem quite compatible with gross licentiousness, and such social courtesy is much more
suggested in books like Castiglione's *Courtier*, of
which Symonds says, 'The principle upon which
these precepts of conduct are founded is not eti-
quette or fashion, but respect for the sensibilities
of others.' Nevertheless, when one surveys the art
and the literature and the historical record of
Renaissance Italy as a whole, one cannot help
divining a rather profound and thoroughgoing
sexual corruption, and indeed what else could be
expected of a world in which the social example was
set by Alexander VI and the Medicis, not to speak
of many other sovereigns? Virtue was a jest,
love-making was a game, and in the temporary
absence of the still greater excitement of bloodshed,
no other game could so lightly and so gayly diver-
sify life.

Into such a world as this Cæsar Borgia was
thrust as a mere boy, with the passions of his tremendous physique, with every inducement and
every opportunity, with family examples of every
sort before him, and with apparently no restraint
either theoretical or practical. Also he appears to
have inherited the peculiar and almost fatal attraction for women which is universally noted in his
father the Pope. What wonder that Cæsar widely
and wildly indulged in all the dissipations which his
wealth and his position could offer him? As to the
detail of these dissipations facts are utterly unob-
tainable and they cannot be separated from what is

probably or obviously legend. That Cæsar had various illegitimate children is undisputed. The darker stories about his relations with his sister Lucretia are generally rejected, though no one can prove or disprove them. There seems little doubt that his sister-in-law Sancia, a gay and frolicsome lady, was for some time his mistress, and there are innumerable suggestions of others. The wealth of variety in this regard is perhaps well covered by Cæsar's haughty remark, when he was charged with the kidnaping of a Venetian lady who was in reality carried off by one of his officers, that he could have all the women he wanted without going to such trouble as that. The celebrated banquet of the nude dancing courtesans, at which Alexander, Cæsar, and Lucretia were present, the episode of the forty young women captives in Capua, and the still darker history of Astorre Manfredi, are merely illustrative features in the more or less mythical garland which Cæsar managed to wreathe about his memory. But it may at any rate be safely assumed that there were few phases of sexual experience with which he was not familiar before he was twenty-five.

That is, sexual experience from the physical point of view. I find not the faintest suggestion of a hint anywhere of love in its emotional, or poetical, or imaginative aspect. The high-wrought, intellectual, analytical raptures of Petrarch were not so very much anterior to Cæsar. Such raptures must have been in the thought of many men and women of

that day, and they certainly reappear again in the
sonnets of Michael Angelo. But if Cæsar Borgia
knew anything of love's longing, or doubt or desolation or despair, he has left us no record of it, unless we may accept as such the love-song which is
said to have been a favorite with him:

> Donna, contra a la mia voglia
> Mi convien da te partire.

Symonds says of Cellini's statues, 'Their blank
animalism corresponds to the condition of their
maker's soul,' and again of the same Cellini, 'He
never rises above animal appetite.' Assuredly the
same might be said of Cæsar Borgia.

Nor is there anything whatever in the circumstances of his marriage to the French princess,
Charlotte d'Albret, to contradict this view. The
minute he threw off the irksome clerical habit, he
and his father began to look about for a matrimon-
ial alliance which would advance his worldly fortunes. He tried the Neapolitan royal family, but
was rejected because of the circumstances of his
birth. In France he was more successful and when
he went to arrange a marriage there, it was with
every circumstance of splendor. Charlotte was a
beautiful and noble woman, and it must be said to
Cæsar's credit that he seemed to appreciate her,
at any rate to treat her with a courtesy and respect
which completely won her heart. But he remained
with her only a short time, long enough to become
the father of one daughter, born after his depart-

ure. Then he returned to Italy, leaving his wife behind, and she ceased to affect his life, if indeed she ever had affected it.

For the important thing about Cæsar Borgia is that, much as he had to do with women first and last, no one of them seems to have influenced him in the slightest. His attitude was wholly that of Enobarbus in *Antony and Cleopatra:* 'Though it were pity to cast them away for nothing, yet as between them and a great cause they should be esteemed nothing.' In this regard Cæsar was far different from his father. Perhaps even Alexander hardly allowed the larger course of his life to be swayed by women, but certainly Vanozza Catanei and later the gorgeous Julia Farnese, whom the mocking Romans called 'the Spouse of Christ,' played a far larger part in it than Cæsar ever permitted to fall to the lot of any woman. He picked what women had to give him like fruit or flowers and threw it away unregarded, which gives all the more point to the concluding sentence of Anatole France's comment upon him, with its somewhat exaggerated allusion to the devastating results of his vicious indulgence: 'He had a profound contempt for women.... Nobody ever knew even the name of the mother of the two bastards whom he left behind him. It may justly be said that he never considered a woman worth a thought. Yet this creature of magnificent strength lost in one day by means of a woman all his health and all his beauty.'

CÆSAR BORGIA

It is likely that Cæsar did not care much more for men than he did for women. The charm of his appearance and manner was great and prevailing and in early years he seemed to give free way to it. How great his attraction could be appears in the account of one who was close to him: 'He is a personage of a lofty spirit, very superior, and of an exquisite character. His manners are those of one of high birth, his temperament is cheerful and full of gayety, there is an atmosphere of joy about him.' But one cannot help suspecting a certain amount of policy in even this early joyousness when one considers the later development. For as the years went on, Cæsar seemed to conclude that he would best assert his greatness by retirement, reserve, and secrecy. More and more he cultivated the habit of living to himself, not only socially, but keeping his counsel and imparting his plans to no one until it became absolutely necessary. It was difficult for even important ambassadors to get access to him and no one understood better that rarity of intercourse heightens the value of it. Machiavelli says of the general atmosphere of reserve: 'There is an admirable secrecy observed at this court, and no one speaks of things respecting which silence is to be observed.' And he adds more particularly of Cæsar himself: 'I should moreover observe to your Lordships that his Excellency is not accessible except to two or three of his ministers, and to such strangers as may have important busi-

ness to transact with him.' He loved to keep unusual hours and to receive even dignified visitors
stretched quietly on his bed. Yet with all this, the
charm continued to the end when he chose to
exercise it.

His personal relations with his family are not
much easier to disentangle than the more general
ones. One would like to know more about the
mother Vanozza and her influence, if she had any.
From some things she did one would infer character
as well as beauty. But the Pope preferred to have
his children brought up by an aristocratic relative
and their contact with their mother appears to have
been irregular. The most striking incident in this
connection is the general banquet which Vanozza
gave to all her children on a summer night in 1497.
For on that night, after they had all assembled, as
it seemed in affectionate gayety, the Duke of
Gandia and Cæsar rode away together, and Gandia
was never seen alive again. But what Vanozza
thought and felt and said about it all we shall never
know.

Nor is there much more light upon Cæsar's relations with his brothers. The youngest one, Giuffredo,
seems to have been comparatively insignificant and
is chiefly conspicuous for the hilarious doings of his
jovial wife Madame Sancia, who bestowed her favors rather indiscriminately upon everyone but her
husband, and was at least suspected of being on
good terms with both of her husband's brothers.
Jealousy in this connection may have made Cæsar

hostile to Gandia. Also, the latter was at first evidently preferred by the Pope and seemed to have
the lead in all matters of temporal preferment.
Whether this would have been sufficient to induce
Cæsar to take active steps to get rid of his brother,
no one can say. If he did take such steps, he was
assuredly a master in concealing them, but his mastery in this regard was manifest in almost every
detail of his life. There is less doubt about his
agency in the murder of his sister's second husband,
the Duke of Bisceglie, though the motive is not so
obvious as in the case of Gandia. Bisceglie was
first assaulted on the steps of the Vatican by a company of ruffians. When he seemed likely to recover
from this, Cæsar made his way to his apartment,
turned out Lucretia and Sancia, who endeavored to
protect the invalid, and put him into the hands of
one of his own subordinates who was an adept at
strangulation. The excuse was that Bisceglie was
seeking Cæsar's life.

Cæsar seems always to have regarded his sister
Lucretia with a peculiar tenderness. Lucretia's
historical fate, as well as her actual, has been a
rather hard one. For years she was held up as a
monster of iniquity. The German historian Gregorovius endeavored to exonerate her from the
worst charges. But the best that can be said for her
is that she was a pale puppet in the hands of her
father and brother, who married her and unmarried
her to suit their political convenience. Gregorovius's attempts to establish her virtue remind one

irresistibly of Ariosto's comment on his peregrinating heroine and her asserted chastity:

Forse era ver, ma non però credibile.

It may have been true, but it is quite incredible.

Like some other superannuated ladies, she died substituting the love of God for the love of man.

Cæsar's relation with his father is more tangible if not more engaging. Alexander was a more outspoken person than his son, or at any rate cultivated the appearance of being so. Furthermore, he was devoted to his children and was ready to sacrifice the welfare of the whole Christian world for their benefit or even their pleasure. The man is admirably painted in the remark of one of the ambassadors at his court: 'The Pope... is seventy years old; he grows younger every day, his cares do not last a night; he is of cheerful temperament and only does what he likes; his sole thought is for the aggrandizement of his children; he troubles about nothing else.'

The Pope did not hesitate to find fault with Cæsar. He complained of his extravagance, he complained of his vehemence, he complained of his bloodthirstiness. But he adored him, and, what was more important, he came more and more under his influence, even to the extent of the extremely dubious policy of supporting him in the French alliance against the Spanish. When one weighs the two characters side by side, it is difficult to say which was the stronger. Cæsar was certainly more impetuously dominating and masterful, but it may be that Alexander had the clearer and more far-reaching intelligence. Only intelligence succumbed to will, as so often happens, especially when the intelligence is obscured and led astray by engrossing affection. As to Cæsar's love for his father, it is hard to believe that it went very deep. The most illuminating incident in regard to it is his despicable appearance in the scene of his humiliation before his enemy Guidobaldo, which I have before referred to, when he laid 'the blame upon his youth, his evil counsellors, his bad companions, the abominable disposition of the Pope and of some others who had urged him to that undertaking, entering into many details concerning the Pope, and cursing his memory.' Not a very pretty performance, but who shall say how much was real, if the words were ever spoken, and how much was put on for a purpose?

If Cæsar had no great regard for his father, there is no particular reason to suppose that he had any great regard for anyone else. It was said that he cherished a certain amount of affection for the friends and teachers of his youth and he was disposed to favor them in later years as far as he could without inconvenience. But it cannot be shown that he was dominated or controlled or even influenced by any human being, and when his satellites ceased to be useful or dared to controvert him in any way, they suffered for it, as in the case of his deputy-governor, Ramiro de Lorqua, who was an efficient minister of justice, but offended the people by his cruelty and finally offended his master in some mysterious manner, and therefore was found one morning cut to pieces in the open market-place as an awful example.

Yet, with all this austerity and severity, there is no question as to Cæsar's power of attaching men as well as women. He had a general popularity which is difficult to understand, so that an historian by no means overfriendly to him says that 'he was greatly beloved, not only by the men of war, but also by many people in Ferrara and in the States of the Church — something which seldom falls to the lot of a tyrant.' Moreover, his immediate followers were so devoted to him that even in the bitter hour of his downfall they clung to him and refused to give up the towns and forts they were holding for him till they were absolutely compelled to do so. He had in his nature the mysterious something that draws and holds souls, and he made the most of it.

If Cæsar was not very ardent in loving, it may be said that he was at least a vigorous hater, but even here the doubt may be raised, whether his hate was a blind emotional animosity or was not merely a cold, unrelenting determination to get out of his way any thing and any person that opposed him or thwarted him. Certainly obstacles of this kind were removed, at once and forever, with a singular and fatal ingenuity of quiet and deadly destructiveness. And as Cæsar was perhaps not a hater for hate simply, so it hardly seems that he loved bloodshed for itself with any sort of sadistic gloating, though he did not stop at rivers of it when required by his purposes. There are dubious stories about his looking on in secret at one of his strangler Michelotto's executions, and of his letting loose a group of prisoners in a courtyard and then shooting them down with bow and arrows for the delectation of his father and Lucretia. But in general he preferred to leave the strangling and torturing to be done in his absence, as with his brother-in-law and with the rebels at Sinigaglia, whom he lured into the trap with his Judas caresses and then turned over to Michelotto to be disposed of.

Yet, whether he reveled in actual killing or not, you have to recognize in him, as in so many Italians of the period, a singular indifference to human life and death, which seems to grow up curiously, something as it is doing today, among those to whom the life of this world has become all and yet at the same time almost nothing. And I ask myself, among the many puzzling questions with regard to Cæsar, whether this was really his theoretical attitude, whether he argued deliberately that a dream existence in a dream world was of little account to him or to anyone, or whether, as is far more likely, the universe seemed to be so vastly centered in one real life, that of Cæsar Borgia, that all these other shadows were insignificant and merely to be trifled with and tossed about and got rid of as shadows should be. The latter view is most powerfully and profoundly suggested in a remark of Machiavelli: 'I do not know whether it will be easy for me to obtain audience of the Duke, for he lives only to advance his own interests, or what seem to him such, and without placing confidence in any one else.' In other words, all men and all women, and all circumstances, were to be used and handled and indeed existed only for the exaltation and the gratification and the wider satisfaction of Cæsar Borgia.

v

After which it need hardly be said that God existed for exactly the same purpose. From his infancy Cæsar grew up with the idea that the Church, that is, the supreme manifestation of God in this world, flourished largely to advance and benefit him. Without the slightest merit or effort on his part the highest ecclesiastical dignities were heaped upon him. He was made a bishop, he was made a cardinal; best of all, the solid financial accessories of these titles and grandeurs flowed in upon him and supplied him always with abundant means for his pleasures and his ambitions. No doubt he went through the round of Church observances and ceremonies as they came to him, but what idea he entertained of a God who was served in that fashion it is difficult to conjecture. Perhaps he did not entertain much of any.

Nor is it to be supposed that in this religious, or irreligious, attitude he was different from at any rate a great many churchmen of his day. For a thousand years the Church had been a great temporal power, with unlimited wealth and unlimited intriguing worldly influence. It was inevitable that the chief places in it should often be filled by men to whom the affairs of this world were everything. No doubt there were plenty of spirits of another type, lofty, pure, ideal souls to whom this world was dross and horror. As one of the cardinals contemporary with the Borgias expresses it: 'When I think of the life of the Pope and the lives of some of the cardinals, I shudder at the thought of remaining in the Curia.' Unfortunately, the handling of this world's affairs naturally fell to those of the more worldly order. And of that order it would be difficult to find a more complete example than Alexander VI. As Head of the Church he was a great temporal sovereign, and no sovereign of his day or any other day ruled with a more entire absorption in the end of personal power or a more complete willingness to resort to any means by which that end might be attained. Yet it would probably be a mistake to charge Alexander with a too deliberate hypocrisy. He believed in God, believed in the truths of Christianity, as he saw them, believed that he had been appointed to represent God in this world's matters and that he must manage them as they must necessarily be managed for God's greater glory. Even the solemn and terrible words with which he presented the Golden Rose to his bastard son Cæsar, whom many would regard as the greatest thief and blackguard in the world except himself, were probably sincere to him in a sense: 'Accept this mystic rose, bedewed with balm and musk, typifying the sweet odours that should exhale from the good deeds of us all, especially of those in high places. Accept it, well-beloved, who in the temporal order art noble, mighty, and endowed with great power, and may virtue grow in thee ever as a rose planted beside rivers of water, which grace may He who is Three in One for all eternity vouchsafe to grant you out of His abounding loving-kindness.' To Alexander and Cæsar and their like the Church was a great business proposition and it is so extraordinarily easy to believe in anything which gives us an income!

One asks one's self how much of the religious emotions, hope, fear, or love, there may have been under this mask of current business and tradition. No doubt there were many, many sensitive souls who were touched by these things, as they always have been and always will be. It was not so very many years since the 'Imitation' was written in a Northern monastery, and the 'Imitation' was then, as it still remains, the most perfect flower of religious ecstasy. And there were times when, in spite of the involving atmosphere of business, even the most worldly were moved and shaken. Take Alexander himself, who must remain the typical and terrifying example. After the death of the Duke of Gandia, the Pope, his father, that robust, sturdy, solid, immensely animal and animally emotional nature, went through a most instructive crisis of grief and remorse. For several days he shut himself in his own apartment, whence cries and groans of paternal agony were constantly heard. When he appeared in the Curia, it was at first to break out in the most extraordinary scene of self-reproach. He had sinned, and now he was punished. The Church was woefully, direfully corrupt. It must be reformed and he would devote his declining years to reforming it. And he at once appointed a Commission for that purpose. Yet in a few hours the old man began to peep out and he instinctively appointed on the Commission his own creatures, who would be sure to report nothing that would involve the Borgias in disgrace. When the report finally came, it was decently laid on the shelf, the Borgias were themselves again, and grief, repentance, and reform were forever forgotten.

We get no such sudden, tremendous storms as this in Cæsar, nor is there any real suggestion of mystical ecstasy or interest in him. It is, indeed, said that he kept by him a Spanish Life of Christ. I wonder if he read it. Spanish in his tastes and habits as he undoubtedly was and not incapable of Lowell's hints of Spanish chivalry,

> O life borne lightly in the hand,
> For friend or foe, with grace Castilian!

there is nothing whatever of the ideal mysticism which developed a hundred years later in Calderón.

The truth is, it is curious to trace in this Italian

Renaissance the constant, almost pervading theoretical, mechanical, presence of God together with his spiritual and especially moral absence. One gets the sense of the contradiction all through the great poem of Ariosto and still more in the cruder *Morgante Maggiore* of Ariosto's predecessor Pulci. Pulci invokes the Deity and all the celestial personages in his opening stanzas to every canto with the most familiar and intimate devotion and then introduces them to scenes as grotesquely incongruous as would be furnished by the novels of Boccaccio. Take another artistic form, the sculptural tombs of many of these great churchmen. They are laid out with folded arms and lifted eyes in all the deepest attitude of reverence and devotion, but those desperately veracious Renaissance sculptors carved the cardinals and the bishops with faces full of greed and lust and cunning, just as they were through all the rush and hurry of their base and sordid earthly lives. And again the great Alexander is the crown of it all. What were his morals? What could he possibly have thought them? The categorical imperative, the great 'Thou Shalt Not,' had been completely swept away. The one law was to do as you pleased, as Alexander pleased, the one limitation, expediency, the measure of your own physical strength and your capacity to achieve and to enjoy.

But the consideration of Cæsar's moral attitude is far more interesting than that of Alexander's, because we gather that Cæsar was more reflective and analytical by nature. To be sure, those dark and mysterious depths are largely hidden from us, just as, after all, the deepest recesses in our own souls are hidden even from ourselves, but there are hints and gleams with Cæsar that are richly suggestive. Thus one of his most apologetic biographers tells us of a ring he had made, which bore as a motto on the inside, 'Do your duty, no matter what happens,' and on the outside, 'One heart, one pathway,' and the biographer deduces that Cæsar had secret stores of conscientiousness not generally divined. But I confess I cannot help thinking of George Ade's discontented married couple. 'The motto on the dining-room wall said, "Love one another," but they were too busy to read.'

Again, one wonders whether Cæsar made excuses to himself or whether he deliberately wrapped himself in a lofty moral indifference. He made excuses to others whenever it suited him. Machiavelli cites several of these, most specious and ingenious, and quite calculated to impose upon those whom he was scheming to deceive and to betray, as his remark in regard to the Bentivogli: 'His Excellency said, furthermore, that he had been very glad to conclude the treaty with the Bentivogli; that he wanted to act towards them as a brother, and that God Himself had had a hand in bringing about that treaty.' Whenever there was a question of external argument, he was right, morally, and the other fellow was wrong. What went on within we shall never clearly know, but we may conjecture pretty definitely that in the murky doubt involving all issues, human and divine, the will of Cæsar Borgia was a better guide than any other, and the dominant, aggressive, all-engrossing personality of Cæsar Borgia was the one thing in this world that counted. As for the other world, with all its shadowy possibilities, which had brooded so heavily and vastly over the mediæval time, I find no evidence that it meant anything to Cæsar whatever, any more than it meant anything to Theodore Roosevelt or Nikolai Lenin.

VI

So we return to the Renaissance, with its rediscovery of the life and the pleasures and the excitements and the passions of this world. The peculiar and fatal thing is that a too great preoccupation with the life of this world, for the average man, is apt to result in the predominance of the senses and the animal instincts. The privileged few may turn to the pleasures of the imagination and the intelligence, but the many are apt to run riot in delights that, as the old poet says, are sweetened in the mixture but tragical in issue.

So under all the imaginative glory and splendor of the Renaissance the animal life was lurking and with time it became increasingly evident. It is curious to trace the progress in the painters. The mediæval superearthly tradition still lingers in the primitives. When we come to Botticelli, it is extraordinary and fascinating to trace the tortured blend of spiritual motive with earthly influence, and there is no more curious or subtle psychological study than the consideration of the face of Botticelli's Venus, the goddess of love and earthly desire with all the vague longing and spiritual restlessness of the Middle Ages still lingering in her eyes. As we go on with Raphael and the Venetians, this world declares itself more and more, and at last in the fleshly splendors of Rubens we have the animal flaunting its sensual ardor naked and unashamed.

In the same way, it must be admitted that the great Elizabethan drama, culminating in Shakespeare, is a drama of this world, saturated with the glory and the richness of the sensual life, as the great Venetian painting is. The outcry of Macbeth,

> Life is a walking shadow, a poor player
> That struts and frets his hour upon the stage
> And then is heard no more. It is a tale
> Told by an idiot, full of sound and fury,
> Signifying nothing,

may be put aside as the wail of a guilty soul, but the dream-reverie of Prospero is equally nihilistic:

> And, like the baseless fabric of this vision,
> The cloud-capp'd towers, the gorgeous palaces,
> The solemn temples, the great globe itself,
> Yea, all which it inherit, shall dissolve
> And, like this insubstantial pageant faded,
> Leave not a rack behind. We are such stuff
> As dreams are made on, and our little life
> Is rounded with a sleep.

35

As has been well said of the Elizabethan dramatists as a whole: '*They* had no questionings about the future, no quarrelings about dogmas, no beliefs or disbeliefs. But then they were not Christians, oh, not the least bit Christians. Human life was enough for them, this world with all its joys and all its griefs, the red heart-beat of passion, the honey-sweet of love, the blind pulsation of revenge, the fierce struggle of ambition, the dead languor of sated desire — all these they knew and painted, gods! in what a language! With what came after they did not seriously trouble themselves.'

The interest of all this is that the America of the twentieth century seems also to be giving itself to the life of this world, as did the Renaissance. The difference is that the imagination does not figure so gloriously now as it did then. On the other hand, there is a far clearer and more definite rejection of the other world than the Renaissance in general ever ventured upon. The Renaissance simply left the other world on one side, contentedly absorbed with the issues of splendor that daily surged up about it everywhere. The twentieth century deliberately dissolves the other world in the vast emptiness of space and time and insists that happiness and satisfaction must be found if at all anywhere in the full development and self-expression of the individual right here.

The peculiar interest of Cæsar Borgia is that he carried out this view of things with special advantages of inherent physique and external opportunity which the youth of the twentieth century may envy but can hardly equal. As Anatole France puts it, of the Borgias generally, 'these Romanized Spaniards were not born, so far as we know, with a different heart or a different soul from the common run of men.... There is not one small office in our great cities that does not contain within its four walls... all the lusts and all the hatreds that burned in the Vatican under the Spanish Papacy.' When the joyous youth of today proclaims the sacred right to indulge its instincts without trammel or restraint, it is just as well to turn back to the Italy of the fifteenth century through which rides and revels the mysterious, dominating, superbly self-asserting figure of the Duke of Valentinois, who gratified his passions without scruple, bullied his father, murdered his relatives, outraged man, and defied God, thus affording a delightful example of the inherent privilege of self-expression and the free development of spontaneous individual instincts in the glad and golden days of the Renaissance.

II

GOD'S VAGABOND
SAINT FRANCIS OF ASSISI

CHRONOLOGY

Francesco Bernardone.
  Born, Assisi, 1182.
  Repaired San Damiano and quarreled with father,
    1206.
  Discovered vocation, 1209.
  Pope Innocent approved Rule, 1209.
  Went to Egypt, 1219.
  Returned, 1220.
  Resigned headship of order, 1220.
  Received Stigmata at Alverna, September, 1224.
  Composed Canticle to Sun, 1225.
  Died at La Portiuncula, October 3, 1226.

THE MYSTIC MARRIAGE OF SAINT FRANCIS OF ASSISI
WITH CHASTITY, POVERTY, AND HUMILITY
By Pietro di Sano

II

GOD'S VAGABOND
SAINT FRANCIS OF ASSISI

I

IN THIS developing twentieth century the immediate world of space and time has become so ample, so rich, so varied, in its hurrying, crowding luxury of interest and splendor, that it seems to absorb and engross us altogether, especially as the sense of any other world has grown more and more obscure and dim. It is, then, surely curious and perhaps profitable to turn back seven hundred years to a man like Francis of Assisi, to whom the things of the other world, eternal things, were so vivid and so real that he literally cast the joy and the splendor and the glory of this world under his feet and trod them in the dust.

Francis Bernardone, born about 1182, was the son of a well-to-do traveling merchant of Assisi. He was brought up in ease and luxury and seemed at first disposed to dissipation and riotous companionship. But he had a tender heart and a vivid imagination. These things soon made him sensitive to human misery, and above all keenly alive to the injustice of his having the good things of the world while so many others were wholly without them. Since his mind was as logical as his heart was sym-

41

pathetic, the next step was to discard his own advantages utterly, and to stride right out into the empty world with the spirit of Christ as his only possession. Rich in this, he preached Christ, he practiced Christ, he lived Christ, and with the aid of the Church and of those in authority, he established an order of followers, whom he sent out from his little chapel in Assisi to preach the gospel as he saw it, all over the world. He himself, after two unsuccessful attempts, got as far as the Orient, in 1219, in the track of the Crusaders, and preached the gospel to the heathen and even to the Sultan, though without converting him or attaining the ideal of martyrdom which seemed so desirable. When Francis returned to Italy, the aura of sainthood had already gathered about him, and his death in 1226 is enveloped in the usual cloud of unprofitable miracles, culminating in the mysterious Stigmata, or impress of Christ's wounds upon the saint's body, a cloud of myth and legend from which it is almost as difficult to disentangle the real man as in the case of Jesus himself. Yet Francis, like Jesus, was so vividly and intensely human that even the adoration of seven centuries is not enough to obscure him entirely.

The first principle of Francis's religion was that of absolute, complete, uncompromising poverty. It seemed to him that not only the possession of money, but the desire for money and what it brings, was the root of all evil. And it is difficult not to agree with him that if you could get rid of that desire, most social and economic evils would settle themselves. Modern society, all human society, is composed of a few people who have a great deal, and who incidentally always want more than they have, and a vast number who violently, passionately want what belongs to, or, at any rate, is in the possession of, the others. If you could once thoroughly eradicate the fatal wanting, all the economic problems would be settled. Get rid of it, want nothing but Christ, said Francis. Seven hundred years later Tolstoy adopted much the same attitude. But Tolstoy hardly attempted to get beyond this world, while Francis had the immense compensating possibilities of the other world to support him. Naturally the abolition of wanting involves all sorts of contradictions and inconsistencies. Life would appear to be wanting and the abolition of wanting would come perilously close to death. Furthermore, if nobody has anything, who is to give to others, and how is the world to go on? But Francis had a practical and concrete mind. He did not foresee the slightest danger that the world in general would adopt his principles, and if it did, the world must take care of itself. He saw what was right for him, and he was going to do it, if the heavens fell.

When I was twenty and was engaged to be married, my love and I came to see the world for the time something as Saint Francis saw it. We, too, felt that we should give up luxury and wanting, should discard the comforting equipment of material life, to which we were accustomed, but of which so many millions were destitute, and adopt voluntary poverty for the good of the world and our own souls. As a letter of that time expresses it: 'We should give up everything, live not only simply, but in poverty, with the poorest of clothes and the simplest of food, giving up everything material, everything tending to outward things, not because we want to be ascetic, but because we will have nothing to draw us from the life within and because we want to set an example of forgetting all the luxuries and comforts of the body. We want to build a little house somewhere, perfectly plain and poor, and live there in every way just as peasants would live.'

We were twenty, and simple, and foolish. Our parents and relatives and friends ridiculed us and scolded us and reasoned with us, and in the end forced us to let our ideals go — for better, for worse? — I wonder. The only point of importance is that Francis of Assisi did not let his ideals go; he let father and mother and home and wealth and friends all go hang, and followed God. When his father argued with him and bullied him and finally dragged him before the bishop to be rebuked for taking what did not belong to him, Francis came quietly into the assembled throng, tore off even every rag of clothing and threw it down at his father's feet, declaring that from that day on he had a father in heaven who would provide for him. There are times when I wish I had behaved as Francis did.

SAINT FRANCIS OF ASSISI

He had no doubts or hesitations or difficulties. Or if he had them he overcame them by the goodness of God. As for money, he spurned it, rejected it, cast it from him, from the beginning to the end. As the *Speculum Perfectionis* has it, 'Francis, the true friend and imitator of Christ, despising all things which are of this world, above all detested money and by word and example led his followers to flee it as if it were the Devil.' They were to subsist by God's loving support, and if they relied upon it, it would not fail them. This does not mean that Francis advocated direct beggary as the entire means of livelihood. On the contrary, he was always insistent upon honest labor. Those who followed him should work as they had been accustomed to do and should receive proper reward for it. Only the reward should not go beyond the bare means of subsistence, and, if there was any superfluity, it should be immediately passed on to those who were in greater need.

For Francis not only condemned and contemned money in its immediate form. He was still more hostile to the accumulation of it in possessions of any kind. No radical of the present day could be more bitter in his denunciations of capital, not only in its far-reaching aspects of vaster ownership, but even, perhaps still more, in the petty grasp on small visible holdings to which men cling with a madder grip than they extend to airy claims which they cannot see but only imagine. The owner of a cottage or a cow is a capitalist just as much as is a

Rockefeller or a Ford, and he hates to have the cow or the cottage taken away from him, just as they would hate to lose their millions. All wrong, says Francis, and he speaks right out about the whole business: 'I don't want to be a thief, and to have what others lack is to be a sheer thief and nothing else.' Those who followed him were to count nothing as belonging to them except the clothes on their backs, and even those were often to be turned over to any who might be more greatly in need of them.

Evidently Francis was starting the greatest fight in the world, the one that all fundamental reformers have undertaken, the fight against human nature. Even before his death he saw the huge forces of greed and avarice, the desire for gain and the desire for power, breaking in on the Rule he sought to establish. Over and over he enjoined upon his disciples that they must keep the simple principles before them — love, quiet, faithful labor, persistent self-sacrifice, above all the fundamental idea of not wanting, not wanting the things of this world, rooting them out of your spirit altogether. Poverty, living without money, and all the accursed things which money brings, which cannot be had without it and are of no real profit when you get them, that was the lesson that he tried to teach, by preaching and by example. And with the high-wrought, lyrical, imaginative touch that makes so much of his charm, he breaks out into a hymn of rapture to his spiritual bride, our Holy Lady Poverty: 'To trample under foot is to condemn, and Poverty tramples all things under foot, therefore she is queen of all things. But, oh, my holy Lord Jesus Christ, pity me and my Lady Poverty, for I am tortured with the love of her, nor without her can I find repose.... Oh, who would not love this Lady Poverty above all others? Of thee, dear Jesus of the Poor, I ask to be honored with this privilege, to be enriched with this treasure, that it may be the eternal distinction of me and mine in thy name to possess nothing whatever under heaven of our own, but to be sustained always by the scanty use of others' benefits, so long as this miserable flesh endures.'

Undeniably in these raptures and vehement assertions and injunctions of Francis there is the touch of extravagance and excess which sometimes repels and estranges. There is the mediæval quaintness of expression, there is the ascetic forcing, which makes you feel the ideal to be elevated beyond human reach. What tempers and sweetens all this in Francis is the peculiar flavor and relish of sympathy and tenderness. When his demands seem most impossible, you feel that his penetrating eyes look right down into your heart and see the weakness as well as the strength. Does not the whole depth of the tenderness shine out in this lovely sentence from a letter of his later years? 'And I shall know whether you love God and me, his servant and yours, if you do this: see to it that there shall be no brother in the world, no matter how much he has

sinned, who if he has once met your eyes, shall go
away without your pity. And if he does not ask
pity of you, do you ask it of him.' No harsh injunction about poverty could ever chill the infinite
loving-kindness of that.

II

The second great fundamental principle of Francis's religion was the principle of obedience, and it
seems hardly likely that this would be any more to
the taste of the twentieth century than the principle of poverty. The vast individualism that has
developed during the last hundred years does not
greatly relish the notion of blind obedience to anyone for any purpose. Yet it must be admitted that
the ideal of obedience is a very restful thing. When
one has struggled long with doubtful courses, anxious above all things to do the right, but utterly
unable to see where the right lies; when one has
come to have a hopeless mistrust of one's reason for
guiding one anywhere and to feel that the responsibility for action is the most terrible burden in the
world, the dream of obedience to someone who will
take all the responsibility and all the burden, to
someone who knows, to someone who even thinks
he knows, is an exceedingly alluring one. Moreover, obedience is one of the greatest agents in the
world for getting things done. The supreme organiz-
ing saints, Dominic, Ignatius, understood this perfectly, and built their world-power upon it. Also,
obedience is the very best training for command,

and those who have formed the habit of taking orders quickly, intelligently, unquestioningly, are often the ones who end by giving the most effective orders themselves.

It may appear that what is apt to be the earliest phase of obedience, the submission to paternal authority, was not very conspicuous in the case of Saint Francis. But as he went on with his life and work, he came to feel that obedience was a most essential virtue, not only for others, but for himself. Great heretics in the religious sphere, like great radicals in the political, are apt to have the instinct of rebellion, even of destruction. They have often the blind impulse to root up and overthrow existing institutions to get rid of their defects, with a secure confidence that the dynamic creative force of mankind will provide something better in their places. The history of Francis's forerunners in that turbulent twelfth century, so effectively told by Miss Davison and Miss Richards, is a history of rebellion at many points. But Saint Francis was by no manner of means a rebel, either by instinct or by practice. Like Abraham Lincoln, he was essentially constructive rather than destructive. He wanted to make over the world, but he wanted to make it over by love, and love does not destroy.

From the beginning of his career he showed his profound respect and submission to the authority of the Church. There might be errors, there might be defects, but such a magnificent power in the world was to be used, not to be battled with. Therefore he approached Pope Innocent III, and Pope Honorius III, and his intimate friend Cardinal Hugolino, who afterwards became Pope Gregory IX, with an inimitable combination of reverent tact and straightforward simplicity, which repeatedly secured for him the permissions and the authorizations he required.

Nor was the obedience or the submission confined to the higher powers or to those whose exalted rank necessarily imposed. Francis enjoined upon all who loved him at all times the profoundest respect for even humble representatives of the Church. They were to be honored and heeded for their office, independent of what they might be in themselves. Even when the hand that ministered at the altar was corrupt and unclean, you were to kiss it, not for what it was, but for what it did. And in the most authentic and undisputed of all his written words, his final Testament, Francis expressly records his feeling on the subject: 'If I had the wisdom of Solomon and should come into contact with the poor parish priests of today, dwelling in their parishes, I would not preach against their wishes. And I would reverence, love, and honor them, and all like them, as if they were my lords and masters.'

Never did Francis miss an opportunity to impress ' this duty of obedience and submission upon all who followed him. In one of his letters to the faithful he writes: 'We should never desire to be above others, but should rather be submissive and subject to every human creature for the sake of God.' It cannot be denied that here, as in other things, there are elements of the fantastic, of extravagance and excess. Such, for example, is his likening of complete and implicit obedience to death, since a dead body at least does absolutely what is required of it. And the story runs that he ordered an erring brother to be buried up to the neck, till death seemed immediately imminent, then asked him if he was dead, and on his agreeing, let him go with the injunction to obey his superiors as a dead man would: 'I want my followers to be dead, not living.' But here again it is not the extreme illustration but the principle that counts.

To Francis there were two roots of the supreme, self-resigning obedience. The first root was intellectual. You were to give up, to eschew, to rid yourself utterly of, the pride and exaltation of your intelligence. There has been endless controversy on this point. It has sometimes been urged that Francis was quite ignorant, even of the Scriptures, that he rejected human learning altogether. On the other side it is answered, with good appearance of reason, that he lived with the Bible and that no one could have so perfectly practiced it who was not intimately familiar with its precepts. As later scholarship inevitably made its way into Franciscan pulpits, as into all others, innumerable pleas and explanations have been offered for departing from the Founder's uncompromising attitude. But that attitude is really simple enough. Francis knew what the pride of the intellect is, knew also its abysmal weakness: he had probably had example in himself of both. Learning and scholarship have their place, and he appreciated that place. But learning and scholarship are always too ready to exalt themselves, and they are of no account when once they are placed in competition with the light and the power of the spirit. Francis lived by the spirit, and he wanted others to do the same.

And as the first root of obedience is the humility of the intellect, the obliteration of intellectual pride, so the second root is the abasement of the will. It is the determination to do things simply because you want to do them that kills. This is what you must root out and tear up and overcome. You are told to go and do things. Go and do them, no matter whether every impulse of poor, fragile human nature rebels or not. You are to face ridicule and scorn and discomfort and torture and death, simply because you are ordered to do so, without debate or dispute or discussion or delay.

After which, even for saints like Francis, or rather supremely for the saints, there remains the qualification that when human obedience grows too distasteful, you can fall back upon the will of God, beside which all human command is dwarfed and insignificant. Thus, when the highest authority of the Church suggested that he should make some alteration in his Rule, Francis gently but absolutely declined to comply: 'I, most Holy Father, did not place those precepts or words in the Rule, but Christ.... Therefore I must not and I cannot change or remove the words of Christ in any way whatever.' For there is degree in obedience as in other things.

Yet all the time I confess that what most appeals to me in Francis's gospel of obedience is the getting rid of responsibility, throwing the burden of settling life upon someone else. It seems to me that this is what I have always longed for, and yet I wonder if, after fifty years of erratic independence, I should really relish it. So, alas, of all Francis's virtues. In him they appear exquisite, but an old and weary body, saturated with this world, might find them onerous in practice. The marvel of Francis is that he practiced what he preached. But then he believed in God and in a future life, and perhaps that makes all the difference.

III

The third great principle of Francis's religion was that of chastity, symbolizing in its most vehement form the conflict between the baser, more animal instincts, and the obedience to the higher, spiritual self, an obedience even more difficult and even more significant than the submission to the external will and commands of others.

As with Francis's other principles, there is something about this one also strange, if not quite repellent, to the whole intellectual attitude of the present day. The growing tendency of the later nineteenth and opening twentieth century is to establish a unified human nature, to recognize all the natural instincts as not only respectable but normal and desirable, not to be fought with and repressed and restrained into unnatural fury and turbulence, but to be directed and guided and developed to their fullest satisfaction, limited only by the simple dictates of expediency and commonsense. It is needless to say that the view of Francis and of his age was totally different from this. The animal elements in our nature were the province of the Devil, at any rate the Devil was given power over us by means of them. It was our duty, our highest religious function and divine privilege, to control and subdue these elements by the power of God working through conscience to a higher, remote, future end, an end conforming to God's will and leading to our own supreme final happiness, beside which the mere immediate gratification of the animal instincts seemed ineffably tame and poor.

At any rate, such self-conquest meant everything to Saint Francis of Assisi. And from the hour of his first conversion his effort was to subdue and overcome the weaknesses of the flesh in every possible way. As to the grosser temptations of sex, there is the strange legend, so much associated with other saints that it is difficult to give it more than a legendary character, of his rushing out naked and burying himself in snow-banks to teach the rebellious passions the indispensable lesson of frigidity. Much more valid and significant are the general comments and warnings as to the danger of association with the opposite sex: 'Dear brethren, we ought to avoid the intimacy, the conversation, even the sight of women, which are the occasion of ruin to so many, all the more zealously when we realize how such things disturb the weak and weaken the strong.'

Yet it is interesting to find that, for all these general injunctions, which no doubt were rigidly applied and acted upon, women played a considerable part in the Saint's life, as was only natural with a temperament so sensitive and so quickly and obviously responsive to all the more delicate emotions. There was the somewhat shadowy Roman lady, Madame Jacopa di Settesoli, to whom Francis seems to have turned for comfort and advice when he was in the Capital and who was opportunely present with him in almost his very last moments. Still more, there was the exquisite Saint Clara, who in her youth cast aside wealth and worldly happiness as Francis did and made it her glory to establish an order of feminine piety in intimate association and affiliation with his. And to Clara even more than to Jacopa, Francis turned for encouragement and inspiration in some of the darkest moments of his career. As Sabatier puts it, in one such moment, 'Clara, by urging him to persevere, instilled into him a new enthusiasm. One word of hers sufficed to restore to him all his energy, and from that time on we find in his life more poetry and more love than ever before.'

But Francis's subdual of the lower instincts extended far beyond any contest of sex. All immediate fleshly pleasures and indulgences were to be rooted out and got rid of, for the mere power of overcoming them, if for nothing else. There were the temptations of good living, warm housing, luxurious habitations, delicate food. Francis's scheme of holiness allowed for none of these things. Others could not have them, and why should you? If by any chance any little rag or shred of comfort came in your way, what better could you do with it than dispose of it to someone who needed it more? The body, this wretched body, which must so soon be food for worms, why cater to it, why pamper it, why caress it? And in his strange, quaint fashion, he sometimes abused it familiarly, chiding it as 'Brother Body'; sometimes he spoke of it as 'the ass,' to be whipped and bullied and made to travel and bear burdens just exactly as its spirit owner might desire.

Doubtless this abuse of the body went to the usual excesses. It was not only denied, it was tormented. Doubtless there were extravagances of penance and self-humiliation which seem almost childish, as when the Saint ate a bit of chicken for the good of his health and then, in an agony of remorse, had one of his followers hale him into church with a rope around his neck to do penance for his weakness. And the abstinence and the privations were destructive to a physique which was never of the best, so that Francis's last years were a story of physical suffering which would be painful to read about if the sufferings were not borne with such complete spiritual tranquillity even to his final death on the bare ground with nothing beneath him but one poor garment.

But the acme and climax of Francis's self-struggle was undoubtedly his experience with the lepers. These unhappy creatures were at that time to be found in Italy in considerable numbers, and of course collected in the usual colonies. Francis had always regarded them with the peculiar horror of a sensitive nature, had pitied them, had been ready to aid them as he could — from a distance — but had shunned all intimate contact with them in instinctive disgust. Then one day, about the time of his conversion, he was riding in the country when a leper came in his way. His first, natural, impulse was to throw the man a gratuity, give him his blessing, and pass by on the other side. But the whole power of the new life that had come upon him said no. Here was the opportunity to show the stuff that was in him at its fullest and richest. He went right up to the leper, not only gave him what he had about him, but embraced him, and treated him in every respect as a brother and a friend. From that hour he felt that he had fought the great fight and won, and ever after the lepers were an object of peculiar tenderness and respect and of his constant injunctions to those who followed him. For the lepers merely symbolized the highest victory that a man can win in this world, the victory summed up in the exquisite phrase of the *Fioretti*, '*perfetta leti-*

zia.... vincere se medesimo,' the victory over self, which, alas, some of us never achieve at all.

IV

It would be an entire mistake to assume that the religious life of Saint Francis was in any way centered in the effort to apply these cardinal principles to himself. On the contrary, his first, unfailing impulse was to extend his rich possession to others, all others. At the same time it would be an equal mistake not to emphasize adequately in him the richness and depth of the inner spiritual life which must always be the perennial source of any inspiration that is imparted.

This inward ardor appears in him from the day of his conversion until the end. It is manifest in every line of the story of the conversion as told by Bonaventure: 'One day, while he was praying thus apart and through intensity of fervor wholly absorbed in God, the image of Christ Jesus crucified appeared to him. At this sight his soul was melted within him and the memory of the passion of Christ was so inwardly impressed upon the bowels of his heart that from that hour, whenever the crucifixion of Christ came into his mind, he could hardly refrain from breaking out into tears and groans.' The height, the ecstasy of mystical rapture penetrates passage after passage of the indisputable writings of the Saint himself, as in this sentence of prayer and exhortation: 'Let us therefore desire nothing else, let us wish for nothing else, let nothing else please us

58

and delight us, except our Creator and Redeemer and our Saviour, the true and only God.' Again and again in the midst of his most active labors, Francis withdrew into himself, buried himself in the solitary communion with his Creator from which alone he could draw the vigor and the power to do his work. Sometimes such isolation had its moments of despair. Demons tormented him, actual external demons as he appeared to think, at any rate demons of doubt and question and hesitating uncertainty, as to his powers, as to his accomplishment, as to his salvation. Then the sweet, compelling, involving rapture of God would once more overcome him, and he would return to the world more than ever determined to give all that was in him to making it over and making it what it ought to be and what God would have it.

For the essence of the man, after all, was action, to be up and doing something, for God and other men. It is charmingly typical that the first manifestation of the religious influence in him was the effort to repair a church. When he saw the house of God tottering to decay, he gave what little money he had to save it, then he went out and begged and solicited, and worked with his own hands and got others to work, till he achieved final and satisfying success. That was the kind of man he was. Prayer and contemplation and adoration were all very well. Nobody could have too much of them — provided they did not crowd out other things. But this was a world of work. You could not live in it without

working. Above all you could not save it without
working, and he was going to work, as long as he had
life in him, to help see that it was saved.

There are winning accounts in the different Lives
of the characteristic frankness with which Francis
laid before his friends the problem as to whether he
should devote his life to prayer or preaching: 'In
prayer we talk with God and listen to him and we
mingle with the angels, leading as it were an angel's
life, whereas in preaching we have to descend to
mortality and, living as a man among men, we have
to think and speak and see and hear human things.'
The truth was, he liked human things, for all his
love of the divine, and when the difficult debate
arose in his soul, he settled it forever by the example
of his Lord and Master. Christ came down from
heaven to preach and teach. Are we not bound to
do all things as he did? 'Therefore it seems to be
the will of God that, casting repose away from us,
we should go forth to labor in the world without
(*intermissa quiete foras egrediamur ad laborem*).'
And he did go forth and labor mightily.

When a man gets to dealing with men, to in-
fluencing them, to acquiring power over them, so
that he can lead them whither he will, it becomes a
matter of singular interest to analyze his sense of
that power and his motive in acquiring it and using
it. In other words, how much of his own personal
ambition, his own glorification, enters into his desire and his effort to benefit his fellows? If it be said
that it is ungrateful and ungracious to probe so

deeply and so closely into the more human and perhaps the baser side of those who have given their
lives to apparently unselfish labor, the answer is
that, if we find them somewhat akin to ourselves,
we shall be better able to imitate them, and also for
some of us there is the further sufficing answer, that
the investigation is profoundly curious. As Sainte-
Beuve said: 'Let us not be afraid to surprise the
human heart naked, in its incurable duplicity, even
in the most saintly.' For the saints, if they really
are saints, are sure to come well out of the trial, and
to be left more lovable and more imitable, if not
more admirable.

There is no doubt that Francis in his youth
cherished dreams of vast and vague ambition and
greatness. He was interested in large projects, he
was interested in chivalry and soldiership and the
chivalric ideal. At one time, when there was strife
between Assisi and the neighboring Perugia, Francis with some of his friends was captured and de-
tained as prisoner in the rival city. His fellow captives wondered at his constant cheerfulness and
contentment. 'Why should I not be cheerful?' he
answered. 'Here, to be sure, we are in prison, but
the day will come when I shall be adored by the
whole world.' The same secure, cloudy, dream confidence seems to have inspired much of the effort
and agitation of his early life.

Then God got hold of him and in appearance at
least he cast all these visions and hallucinations
away. He, the humblest and meanest of God's

servants, had been chosen to do God's work. As he puts it in the *Fioretti*, 'God has called us in his holy Religion for the salvation of the world and has made this bargain between us and the world: that we should set the world a good example and that the world should furnish us a living.' When there was such a mission and such a calling, how could there be any thought of worldly exaltation or glory? The servant of Christ had enough to do to promote the cause of his Lord without thinking of any advantage or future reputation for himself: 'So did this man abjure all glory which did not savor of Christ; so did he pour eternal anathema upon all the adoration of men,' says the adoring biographer. And yet — and yet — one wonders. When you assure an inquiring disciple that you owe such leading position as you may have to the fact that you are 'a greater sinner than anyone else in the whole world,' is there not still a lingering satisfaction in the sense of being the greatest something? When you abase yourself in the depths of humility, is there not always a suggestion of the saying of another distinguished Italian of recent years, Mussolini, 'I am not intoxicated with grandeur; I should like to be intoxicated with humility?' And is there such a great difference in the two intoxications, after all? Again and again in Francis himself we seem to get gleams of this bitter struggle with the devouring, persistent ego which will make its own self-glory out of what honestly means to be the bitterest denial of itself. And is there not the profoundest possible depth of human meaning in the lovely words of Thomas of Celano, who is not generally the loveliest of Francis's biographers? *'Sic totum in laudibus hominum vivimus, quia nichil aliud quam homines sumus.* Thus we live all over in the praises of men, because we are men and nothing else.'

This strain, or perhaps remote savor and relish, of earthly glory appears, or is suggested, in the most active agency of Francis's mission to his fellow-men, his gift of speech. Unfortunately, we cannot judge of this agency as fully as we should wish, since we have no record of what the preacher actually said, but only of some of the effects he produced upon his auditors. It is clear that he was not impressive in appearance — a little, sallow, insignificant person to look at. Yet the minute he began speaking, there was such a pervading earnestness in his words that all sorts of hearers were carried away; 'even the most learned men, weighted and freighted with dignities and glories, wondered at his sermons and were overcome with a profitable awe in his presence.' And it is evident that Francis himself felt the danger in such success. Again and again he cries out that those who would follow him must eschew the vain glory of speech, must use their gifts only to magnify God and to perform wonders in his service: 'Blessed is that servant who does not speak with the hope of reward, who does not take pride in showing his own powers and is not glib in speech, but considers sagely what ought to be spoken and answered.' Yet with it all one realizes perfectly that a sensitive temperament like his must have felt in every nerve the superb exaltation which comes with the power to sway men whither you will by your tongue and your imagination. It is God working through you, no doubt, but it is God working through you and not through anybody else.

And as the sense of power and the exaltation of the ego comes with the exercise of oratory, so with some temperaments it comes in the habit of leadership and the practice of wide and systematic governmental organization. It does not appear that this was so much the bent of Francis as of some others, Saint Ignatius for example. His method and his instinct were rather for quiet labor with individual souls. Yet as his Order grew and his mission developed, the necessity of organization was almost imposed upon him and he met it with the ability of his clear intelligence and the tremendous zeal of his working force. Just how far the different Rules and the organization of the Three Orders, male, female, and lay, as they come to us, are to be attributed to him, it is difficult to say, but it is manifest that he had at any rate large cognizance of them. The thought that he had given to the whole subject is conspicuous in his description of the ideal leader of an order such as he would have liked to see. But what strikes me most here again is the significance of the phrase given to him in the *Speculum Perfectionis*: 'There is no prelate in the whole world who would be so feared by his subordinates as God would make me feared by my brethren if I so wished. But God has given me this grace, to be content with all things as if I were the humblest.' 'Let us not be afraid to surprise the human heart naked, in its incurable duplicity, even in the most saintly.'

And Francis's management and ruling of men was not free from the strain and irritation and friction which such ruling almost necessarily involves. It was obvious that his extreme ideals could hardly become popular or practical without considerable modification. When men of the world, men of affairs and executive capacity, took hold of the Order, they were impelled to modify it, almost insensibly, and even when they were as sympathetic as Pope Honorius and Cardinal Hugolino. Francis himself felt that the modification was inevitable, yet he protested with his whole soul against yielding an inch. The change seems to have chiefly centered in Brother Elias, and it is interesting to see the different views of this figure taken by those who take different views of the Order and its purposes. To the strict followers of Francis, Elias, in spite of his undisputed devotion to Francis himself, is anathema, little short of a traitor, while those who interpret more freely feel that Elias's action really established the Order as a great working power in the world. The main interest of the controversy is that it to some extent distressed and darkened the last days of the Saint, though Sabatier probably exaggerates this element of tragedy: Francis, after all, was born joyous and with an enduring confidence in the triumphant goodness of God.

What is most interesting in Francis's human relations is not his larger executive efforts, but his immediate contact with individual souls. Here his touch was instinctive, exquisite, and prevailing. Spirits of diametrically opposite tempers clung to him and adored him with equal devotion. The tender Masseo, the ardent Leo, the volatile Juniper, the haughty Elias, and innumerable others, all alike submitted to that warmly dominating spiritual ascendency. The master understood, he penetrated into the deepest and most hidden corners of men's hearts and saw what went on there and knew and recognized that nothing darker or more shameful went on there than went on in his own. In the simple, direct language of the *Fioretti*, 'As our Lord Jesus Christ says in the Gospel, I know my sheep, and they know me, so the blessed Saint Francis, like a good shepherd, knew all the merits and the virtues of his companions by a divine revelation, and so also he knew their defects.' Like the other great Saint Francis, him of Sales, and like Fénelon, Saint Francis of Assisi was a supreme director of souls, and could turn them into the right way, sometimes by sharp and severe rebuke when it was needed — as when he bade the erring brother, who had soiled his fingers with dirty money, to fill his mouth with ass's dung

—more often by supreme sympathy and the loving, comforting touch, which eases burdens and lightens the dark places, and makes the troubled, groping footing more firm and more secure.

For the man's mission in life was incontestably the gathering and garnering and saving of souls. And if there is a more joyous and more satisfying occupation, I do not know where you will find it. As D. L. Moody, who was perhaps an American Francis, seven hundred years later, expressed it: 'There is no joy in the world like that: the luxury of winning a soul to Christ, the luxury of being used by God in building up his kingdom.' And if Moody and Francis got a certain personal glory out of it, who shall grudge it to them?

v

But the freshest and most delightful of all the elements of Francis's character is unquestionably the impulse of wandering, of joyous, untiring, inexhaustible, vagrant peregrination. It is one of the basic impulses of human nature, perhaps the basic impulse, the desire of new things and fresh experiences, of turning perpetually from one phase of life to another. It is the splendid impulse of youth. Only in most of us the swift flight of years, the clouding conventions of civilized life, the involving burden of social prejudice, numb and kill the original impulse in this case as in so many others. But the sweet, sunny, vagrant ardor crops out at least in the aspirations of the poets, as in the lovely spring cry of Catullus,

> Jam mens praetrepidans avet vagari,

or the wilder murmur of the rash hero of the old dramatist,

> Let rogues be staid that have no habitation;
> A gentleman may wander.

And again there is the musical travel sentence of old Burton, 'For peregrination hath such an infinite and sweet variety that some call him unhappy who never traveled, but beholdeth from his cradle to his old age the same, still, still the same.' Only Burton traveled but in spirit, like so many of us. Francis's restless limbs wanted to waft his spirit all over the world. When he was young, he was fascinated by the wandering dreams of chivalry and knight errantry, and again by the vagrant music of the troubadours, and in later years he used to call his proselyting followers the chivalry of God and used to pour out his religious ecstasies in the troubadour's form.

With this instinct of sweet general vagrancy, with the pleasure of letting one's feet stray whither they will, there is the further delight of varied human contact, of seeing endless human faces, and exploring endless human souls. There was once a social-minded lady who said, 'I should like to meet everybody in the world.' In the same way we feel with the great human poets, the Chaucers and the Shakespeares, the wide love of human nature and human beings, just because they are human. Saint and sinner, doer and dreamer, all are interesting, all are acceptable, because we find something of all of them in our own hearts. The essential elements of this far-traveling human interest are, first, a limitless, inexhaustible curiosity and, second, a considerable indifference to one's own personal comfort; in other words, a constant tendency to forget one's self in the lives of others. And both these elements are undyingly conspicuous in Saint Francis. He had the vast curiosity, the interest in all human souls, where they came from, what their nature was, where they were going to. And he had the instinct, the formed habit of making himself comfortable wherever he might be. To be sure, in later years, he seemed to show a growing attachment to the home center, the Portiuncula at Assisi, and he enjoined upon his followers that they should never forget or desert it. But in the vigorous and active portion of his life, when 'for the space of eighteen years his body never had rest, circulating through varied and far-flung regions,' his principle seems to have been that which he loudly proclaimed, '*Nam ubicumque sumus et ambulamus, habemus semper cellam nobiscum*'; or, in the words of the old poet Donne, holding up the snail as an example,

> Be thou thine own home and in thyself dwell;
> Inn anywhere; continuance maketh hell.

Also, besides the pure pleasure of vagrancy in itself and the interest in humanity, there is the infinite delight in out-of-doors, and this is always evident in Saint Francis. He was willing to meet the crowds in cities, he did not shrink from lepers in body or from lepers in spirit, but what he above all loved was wandering in the fields and woods, the bright air, the broad sky, the sun, the wind, the clouds, and the living creatures inhabiting all this. There is a sunny sweet old play of Richard Brome, called *The Merry Beggars*, which breathes all through it the delicious spirit of vagrancy. The central figure has the charming name Springlove. He is a steward, and a faithful servant, and spends his winter hours over his master's accounts and the tedious minutiæ of daily care. But when spring comes, and the blossoms burst, and the nightingale and the cuckoo begin calling, calling, the blood in Springlove calls too, and he must up and away, leaving master and duty behind him, and follow the cuckoo and the nightingale.

Saint Francis had something of Springlove in his soul, and he too heard the cuckoo and the nightingale when they began their calling. He too felt the charm of the spring flowers and the lure of narrow, winding paths leading perhaps nowhere, or perhaps anywhere. When the call came, he was ready to arise and follow. And he loved all the living creatures and even the creatures that might appear not to have life. With his usual quaint exaggeration, he cherished and reverenced even the stones on which he trod and the water he had to use for washing.

He loved the flowers and the birds and the cicadas. In that strange, unearthly canticle in which he poured out his lyrical, poetical aspiration, he hailed all the works of God with exuberant praise: 'Praised be my Lord God with all his creatures; and specially our brother the sun, who brings us the day, and who brings us the light; fair is he, and shining with a very great splendour: O Lord, he signifies to us Thee!' And there is the delicious story of his preaching to the birds, which appears in so many different forms. When Francis was preparing to discourse one evening out-of-doors, he was interrupted by the mad twitter of the swallows, who gathered in clouds all about him. And at first he smiled and let them twitter. But finally he remonstrated: 'Sister swallows, you might let me have my turn.' And the swallows were suddenly silent, there was not one single twitter, while the Saint held forth to them on the goodness of God.

For all this out-of-doors of Francis is penetrated, permeated with God. It reminds me always of the sweet story of the two young lovers, sitting on an open hillside, watching the light grasses bent all one way in the light south wind, like a group of Fra Angelico angels. And the lady murmured, 'You know, my soul also is swayed gently, like the grasses, in the wind of your love. Only that would make me the flower and you the wind. And I had rather we should both be flowers and God the wind. What could be more exquisite than to be swayed forever hither and thither in the wind of his love?'

It is this pervading presence of God that gives Francis's spirit of vagrancy the final and crowning touch. It is perhaps delicious enough to roam and wander for the pure joy and revel of it. But how much of depth and delicacy and grandeur is added when you feel that it is your duty to wander, that you are called by God to travel over the wide earth, seeing all things, and visiting all men, so that you may enlarge the boundaries of God's kingdom. This is what Francis felt. He lived all his life in the intoxication of it. He imparted the intoxication to thousands who have followed him. Go forth, and do my bidding, and bear my message to the whole wide world. That was Saint Francis of Assisi, God's Vagabond, and prouder in that title than in the glory of kings or the resonant splendor of conquerors. And because the charm of inexhaustible itinerance, physical and spiritual, was blended with the God-impulse, inextricably, the religion of Francis and his preaching have always a singular and delightful touch of joy. There was no gloom about him, no pressure of misery or hell, no touch of asceticism in the tortured sense. As Renan puts it, admirably, 'Note well that Francis forbids us to possess, he does not forbid us to enjoy'; and the experience of humanity, even without Francis, has long ago taught us that possession and enjoyment are by no means identical. Francis wanted his followers to find endless joy in their religion, in their God, and in all the delightful things that their God had scattered about them in such abundant profusion. He was even ready to carry joy to the point of a sweet and sacred merriment, and when Brother Juniper made his careless and trivial jests, Brother Juniper, who is stamped with the magnificent phrase, *'egregius Domini joculator,'* the egregious jester of God, Francis smiled and sympathized, for, he said, 'What are the servants of God but as it were merry-makers who should stir the hearts of men and impel them to spiritual joy?'

So this illimitable roamer and dreamer went on wandering and wondering and loving. With such an inborn tendency, is it not hard to imagine that the wandering should ever stop? Rather you feel that he would go on eternally, traveling, soaring, adventuring, through the vast unplumbed depths of the spiritual universe, always, always, always, touching, enjoying, engrossing — and dominating souls.

III
THE DEVIL'S VAGABOND
CASANOVA

CHRONOLOGY

Giacomo Casanova (de Seingalt).

Born, Venice, April 2, 1725.

Took minor orders, becoming Abbé, 1740.

Escaped from Venetian prison, 1756.

Wandered widely over Europe till 1774.

In England, 1763–64.

Fought Branicki duel, 1766.

Returned to Venice, 1774.

Went to Dux, September, 1785.

First letter from Cécile de Roggendorff, February 6, 1797.

Died, Dux, June 4, 1798.

GIACOMO CASANOVA

III

THE DEVIL'S VAGABOND
CASANOVA

I

To SOME souls, perhaps to many, life is a dull, monotonous routine, just the same dreary daily repetition — sleep, eat, work, play that is duller than work, then sleep once more. And some rebel, and some accept, and some endure, and the tread-mill goes on everlastingly. Other souls again make life a perpetual, bewildering, enchanting adventure, from birth to death, the greatest adventure of all. And some of these are adventurers of the spirit, who, hardly crossing their own thresholds, find or make their existence a delicious tumult of fantastic conjecture and imaginative enterprise, while others stride out with limitless audacity in the material world, wander over the wide earth, tasting love and laughter, the shifting carnival of the senses, and above all the warm contact of men and women — with infinite, undying relish. Of the latter was Casanova. To be sure, his adventure was all on the surface of life, but how varied was that surface, how brilliant, how absorbing! If to some temperaments it would have been unsatisfactory, Casanova's was not one of them.

Giacomo Casanova, or as he later called himself, Casanova de Seingalt, perhaps not very successfully imitating the development of François Arouet de Voltaire, was born in Venice on April 2, 1725. His mother was a beautiful actress, his father was no one in particular, and his family had neither money nor position. But he himself had a quick mind, unlimited self-assurance, and a rabid appetite for the sensual pleasures of life which he managed to keep fairly well satisfied. He was bred for the Church, like Talleyrand, but his tastes were a little too emphatic for that career, even in Italy, and he soon tossed the frock aside and began to live by his wits. After knocking about Venice for some years, he threw himself into the wide world, ranging till he was sixty years old over the whole of Europe, from Paris to Russia, from Turkey to England, from Germany to Spain. In every country and in every capital, where there were women to be made love to and money to be picked up, he found himself at home. In the early fifties he was in Venice and got into prison for months, on political grounds, finally making a miraculous escape, according to his own account of it. Again he resumed his tireless roving, though age began to tell a little, even on him. In 1774 he patched matters up with the Venetian authorities and thought he was going to find repose at last. But his own country did not want him, nobody wanted him, and once more he went a-wandering, till a patronizing nobleman settled him as a dependent in the solitary castle of Dux in Bohemia, where, after a lonely and forlorn old age, he wrote his *Mémoires* and died in 1798, passing, as one of his eulogists naïvely puts it, 'let us hope, to a better life.' He could not well have passed to a worse.

Casanova was a universal lover of women, and, unlike many such, he was nothing else whatever. As Pepys said of himself, 'Which is a strange slavery that I stand in to beauty, that I value nothing near it.' Everywhere the Venetian went the women he wanted seemed to fall into his arms like ripe apples or blackberries. Whether women of real sense and character as well as beauty would have seen through him with contempt is a question. But with the sort he preferred he had rarely any difficulty. He was not exactly handsome; as the Prince de Ligne said, 'he would be handsome, if he were not ugly.' But he was big, he had immense physical vigor, and his tongue had a glibness that bewitched the innocent and fooled the sophisticated. Perhaps his own explanation of matters is the best: 'I had not indeed beauty, but that which goes further, a certain indescribable something which compels regard.' At any rate, regard was what he got, and all sorts, tall and short, light and dark, merry and sentimental, lapsed into his list, some hundreds he says, so that Europe was strewn with bedraggled bits, broken ends, crushed flowers that had dropped from his reckless banqueting.

It does not appear that with this unbounded

sensuality he had any particular taste for the perverse or abnormal. Nevertheless, the amused serenity with which he surveys excesses of this sort in others shows that his abstinence was rather a matter of inclination than of scruple. And the vast lasciviousness of detail with which he describes his feminine experiences would indicate that scruple was the last thing that troubled him. But perhaps the extreme climax of his achievements is the mad orgy of an all-night revel with a girl whom he had good reason to suppose to be his daughter and with the girl's mother at the same time. It may be that I have a little too much of the prudery of old age and of Victorian New England, but it strikes me that not only common decency but even a wholesome indecency must revolt at the cynicism of such a performance as this. Yet I have no doubt half of my feminine readers and even some men will be consumed with curiosity to read the detailed description of it.

But these amorous adventures are of little consequence except for the main and obvious purpose with which they were recorded — or invented — to regale the illicit curiosity of those whose appetite for such things is apparently insatiable. What is of interest to us is rather the man's inner attitude toward his own adventures and experiences. To begin with, was he interested in that attitude, did he analyze and study himself? Evidently he was too busy living to carry such analysis very far. The rush of surface emotions left little time for cool consideration. Still, the reflections recorded or supplied in the *Mémoires* of forty years after show a certain natural proclivity for such things: 'This singular meeting, which offered me the unappreciable advantage of recognizing in myself generous inclinations stronger than my bent for pleasure, flattered me beyond all expression. I was making a great experiment upon myself and knowing that I needed such study, I gave myself up to it with free indulgence.' It sounds genuine, whenever written, and there are numerous other passages of the same kind, though they are pretty well submerged in very different matter.

And in his love affairs one asks how much the man knew of the deeper sides of love as a spiritual emotion. Did he, for example, feel the melancholy, the despair, of satiety, or of rejection, for rejection did occasionally come to him, much to the reader's contentment? There are times when the disturbance of love appears to even him as a scourge and a curse: 'The charms of peace are far preferable to the charms of love; but when you are in love you don't think so.' When his English siren torments him, 'I fortified myself with my good pistols, and I went out with the firm intention of going to drown myself in the Thames by the Tower of London.' But it is all really a bit of comic opera, with the Tower of London in the background, and one's chief impression of these sketchily remembered emotions is that they were consoled with astonishing facility. In his own words, which sound more

genuine than usual, 'Good God! how easy it is
to find consolation when you are in distress.' It
may depend a little upon the seriousness of the
distress and the quality of consolation that will
satisfy you.

Again, Casanova did a good many things others
would have been ashamed of. Was he? There
were moments when even his superb self-confidence
was a little shaken: 'When I thought of the unfortunate Lucie, I thought I experienced remorse
but when I considered M. d'O ——, I really held
myself in horror.' But the horror never seems to go
very deep. It is far, far different from the directly
recorded agonies of Pepys over Deb Willett in the
last volume of the great Diary. In general, Casanova is perfectly ready with his own apologies:
'When at certain moments I cast a glance at my
conduct, I did not fail to find it entirely exempt
from reproach, since after all my libertinism could
at most render me culpable with regard to myself
and no remorse troubled my conscience.' Above
all, one is again struck with the astounding ease
with which all disagreeable reflections are obliter-
ated. The sight of a pretty face, the lure of an insinuating smile, will whiff them away, as a breeze
whiffs unpleasant reflections out of a still pond.

Again, one asks whether in all these varied
amours there is any suggestion of abiding and enduring ideal love. Some hints at times appear to
imply something of the sort, especially before
taking, or in face of persistent rejection. There is

the early tenderness for Lucie, that for Manon in Paris, and for Esther in Holland, and for Pauline in England. And there is the deathbed of Charlotte, who had never been his mistress, with its moment of naïve self-forgetfulness: 'I preferred the sight of that corpse to the whole universe and above all to myself, in my keen affliction not having time to count myself for anything whatever.' Yet again, the almost frightful rapidity with which everything is forgotten, and for the lowest debauchery, seems to make the animal as prominent as ever.

The most charming of the commendations of Casanova's enthusiastic admirers that I have met with is the naïve remark of Mr. Arthur Symons: 'The real man, who perhaps of all others [*sic*] best understood what Shelley meant when he said:

> True love in this differs from gold or clay,
> That to divide is not to take away.'

To me it would appear that Casanova was a complete *reductio ad absurdum* of Shelley's rather nonsensical lines. Being a human animal, he naturally had his gleams of human tenderness, but in general his idea of love was the immediate gratification of the animal instincts on any attractive — or if necessary even unattractive — object that might present itself. I should as soon speak of the true love of a he-goat or a tom-cat. Before Shelley had read a third of the *Mémoires*, he would have been ashamed of his sentiment, if indeed he had ever thought of applying it in such a connection. True love may be arrant nonsense, or it may not be; but nothing would go further to prove it so than the career of Jacques Casanova de Seingalt.

II

Casanova's life was in the pursuit of women and of the means to facilitate that pursuit, as long as his amazing physical vitality was equal to it. When the vitality gave out, he reveled in the memory of his conquests. At the same time he had the natural ability to have done many other things, if he had only had the time. He had brains, quick, keen, eager brains, if not always very profound or very logical. His clerical training had given him the basis of a good classical education, which he never forgot. He was a Greek scholar, a Latin scholar, and he had a remarkable facility in picking up languages as well as in using them. Words were the great agency of his love-making, and he liked to keep a showy and varied stock handy whenever they might be called for. He really loved books, when he was forced into a quiet corner with them, and there were times when he thought books might have afforded him a more tranquil and satisfying contentment than some of his other diversions. Such a passage as the following has a quite genuine ring. No doubt it represented something that for the moment was genuine: 'I passed eight days in that library, which I left only to return home for the night and for the time required for my meals, and I can count these eight days among the happiest of my life, for I was not for one single instant occupied with myself.' But what he called and considered himself soon came forward again, and books and libraries were forgotten.

In the same way the man might have been an author. Indeed, he was an author, and a very considerable one, in quantity at any rate. He translated Homer, he wrote history, fiction, and pamphlets of all sorts, decent and indecent. There were times in his youth when the ambition of writing, as of doing other great things, seemed to appeal to him: 'I was impelled by the desire of making myself celebrated... in the fine arts, or in literature, or in any other honorable career.' But it did not last. Those fatal feminine obstacles, bobbing up at every corner, were too much for him. Goethe, Byron, Heine, were passionate lovers of women, but not one of them would have let a woman stand for a moment in the way of his literary glory or success. To Casanova a petticoat was worth more than a poem at any time.

It was the same with æsthetic interests of all sorts. Casanova on occasion can discuss a picture or a statue quite learnedly. But what was any picture or any statue, compared to the living pictures in the streets? As to music also he had his opinions, but they were abstract opinions, and no doubt he spoke truly when he said, 'music, for which I have never had the least enthusiasm.' If he ever had it, playing the 'cello in a cheap Venetian orchestra destroyed it for good and all. Nor was it any better with nature. This contemporary of Rousseau and Bernardin de Saint-Pierre took no interest in the things that moved them. Birds and flowers and stars might go hang, he wanted men and women. The best he can say of the Forest of Arden, Shakespeare's magical background of *As You Like It*, is, 'In the midst of this immense forest, in which there is not a village to be found and which yet you have to traverse to pass from one country to another, you find hardly anything that is necessary for the comfort of life,' that is to say, not even a presentable woman.

In religion and philosophy Casanova's attitude is mainly that of his eighteenth-century surroundings, one of complete materialism and skepticism. It is all very well to talk about a future life, but the life of the soul here appears to be bound up with the life of the bodily senses, the only life that Casanova cares about, and when those senses are extinguished, why bother about the soul? If there is a God, he stands pretty much in the background, giving way to some mysterious Destiny, or, after all, to pure luck, which is the only goddess this man seriously serves. Yet all the time there are curious and amusing returns to a more conventional attitude. There are moments when the Almighty is treated with patronizing condescension, moments even when Casanova thinks of becoming a monk and retiring from the world. You can easily imagine what moments those are. Also he believes in religion for the people and furiously attacks Voltaire for attempting to destroy the superstitions of the crowd. And as he gets older, he has a queer, morbid yearning for the religion of his fathers, which suggests the conversation of Dumas *père* with his old teacher, when Dumas told him that sooner or later he should desire his prayers. 'But,' objected the gentle old abbé, 'you don't believe in them.' 'No,' said Dumas, 'no, I don't believe in them always, it is true, but be assured, when I need to believe in them, I will believe in them.' Just so might have talked, and for a few moments really felt, Jacques Casanova.

As to morals in the abstract, Casanova's general attitude was much the same as with religion. His theory in the matter was that of the eighteenth century, as well as that of the Renaissance of Cæsar Borgia and of the twentieth century. The old, conventional, supernatural taboos amounted to nothing. We are here in this world with keen senses and a capacity for pleasure; we do not know that we shall ever be anywhere else. Let us seize every bit of pleasure that we can, consistently with keeping up our appetite for it as long as possible and with a very moderate consideration for the comfort of others: 'The philosopher is he who refuses himself no pleasure that does not produce greater pain, and who knows how to discover more.' Curiously enough, as with religion, there is a haunting respect and tenderness for virtue, an occasional tribute to her charms, which is touching if not very convincing, and even a sigh that he has not devoted himself more assiduously to the cultivation of anything so rare. The truth is, he has never had the time.

The special element of Casanova's morals that interests me is the question of his veracity, since that affects the reliability of the *Mémoires*, which on account of their lack of this precious quality appear to me comparatively worthless. Casanova's admirers insist emphatically upon his candor, often confusing, as it seems to me, veracity with nakedness. Why! they urge, does he not tell us he is candid? Like many great liars, he is certainly profuse in his praise of truth: 'I have loved truth with such passion that I have often begun by lying to get it into the heads of those who do not know its charms.' It is a rather perilous method of setting out. Pepys does not praise the truth; he tells it.

To begin with, of course we must recognize that we have not the *Mémoires* as Casanova wrote them. The editions we have are doctored, expurgated, edited in every way, while the original manuscript reposes in the Brockhaus safe, where I think it had better remain undisturbed, unless someone should have the good sense to burn it up. But the unreliability goes deeper than editing, deeper even than the uncertainty of an aged memory scratching shreds together after forty years. The man was possessed to display everything in a rhetorical light, and all the eight volumes are varnished over with a cheap effort at effect.

Take a very prominent feature of the *Mémoires*,

the interminable conversations. Pepys, even writing the same day, rarely sets down more than a quoted word or two. It is true that Casanova tells us he writes often from notes. But he admits that the dialogues are manufactured, and there is not the least need of his admitting it, for it is quite obvious. That is why, to me at least, even at their most lascivious, they are desperately dull. Naturally no man can write four thousand pages about himself without telling something and it is especially the unintentional revelations that are of value. But when you compare this man's production with any of the great truth-recorders, you feel the difference. Just the bare, simple entry in Burr's Diary, 'Four francs for a prostitute and brandy and two for benevolence,' paints the sordid, meager life of the exile of fifty-five in Paris better than a dozen pages of Casanova's tawdry rhetoric.

The most interesting comparison that I have found for Casanova, because the differences are so striking, is the Memoirs of Fanny Burney. Fanny was, as Feste would say, a mouse of virtue; she was the most virtuous little soul that ever lived. Virtue oozed from her at every pore, just as the other thing oozed from Casanova. Fanny could not have told a deliberate lie to save her life, but then she could not tell the truth either, which leaves her in a rather singular position. Her conversations are just like Casanova's, except that they lack the spice of lecherousness, pages and pages of desolate aridity, because they are purely invented. Fanny

was a paragon of virtue, Casanova was a paragon
of vice, but neither of them had much of the scientific instinct of veracity. A page of Pepys has more
value of human fact than a volume of either.

III

As Casanova had the brains to grasp life, so he
had incomparable opportunities of meeting it in all
its phases. Although he does sometimes complain
of shyness, he had about as little of the article as
falls to most human beings, and what he had, he got
rid of. He was at home in courts and camps, on
land and water, in monasteries and in brothels.
Where there were men, and especially women,
there he felt at home, and could make himself at
home, and could talk unlimitedly about himself
and his own adventures, often making his talk en-
tertaining, no doubt, often also tedious, though this
he does not mention.

With all these wide opportunities for meeting
mankind, one asks one's self if Casanova has much
of curious and original interest to tell us. The
answer is, far less than one would expect. He himself insists upon 'my insatiable curiosity to study
men by making them talk.' But the results of the
study are decidedly disappointing. I explain this
by two things. First, there are the tiresome and
ever-present feminine preoccupations. When your
main interest in any social gathering is the thought
of undressing some woman, it leaves your general observation a little blurry. Secondly, when Casanova

wants to study others, he himself is always getting
in the way. No doubt he liked to make other men
talk, but the diversion of talking about himself and
glorifying his own achievements was so absorbing
that everything else had to give way to it. He had
the opportunities of a Pepys, or a Saint-Simon, or a
Lord Hervey, but he did not really have their passionate curiosity about human nature. It is indeed
astounding that a man who had seen so many great
people and so many notable places should have told
us so little about them of any interest whatever,
but it was largely because those plaguy females
were always obstructing his view.

Yet he did meet the great people, there is no
question about it. He talked with Voltaire, and he
apparently kept some record of that conversation,
which makes it a trifle more appetizing. He met
Rousseau, and Crébillon, and fifty other celebrities
in France and everywhere else. Nor was his acquaintance confined to the literary. Kings and
popes and emperors were on friendly terms with
him, or so he would have us believe, and as to the
Pope we distinctly infer that if he had not been
His Holiness, he would have liked to be Casanova.
Frederick, Catherine, the Emperor and Empress of
Austria, the Kings of Spain and France, all were on
the visiting list. Yet it shows how little impression
the man really made on anyone but himself that
his name is not even mentioned in either of the
great and complete honor-rolls of the century, the
correspondences of Voltaire and Horace Walpole.

And another thing that strikes one is that Casanova met all these sovereigns and statesmen, but took no hold on them. He rarely met them more than once. It reminds one of Shaw's remark · about Harris: 'Frank Harris has been in all the great houses — once.' The kings were all polite, all vaguely interested. Then nothing was heard of them further, and after they had made a little more inquiry there came a gentle hint, sometimes followed by an ungentle hint of jail, that the rover had better be getting on his way. The missive from King Louis XV, in suggesting departure, simply indicated that such is 'my good pleasure.' Umph! grumbled Casanova, what about my good pleasure?

With his masculine equals Casanova was not in general on much more friendly terms than with his superiors. The professional hunter of women is accustomed to look upon all men as possible rivals and probable enemies, and this was too much Casanova's natural disposition anyway. His path was strewn thick with quarrels, and his constant emphasis on the fierce and satisfying pleasure of vengeance is not especially attractive: 'Vengeance, a vice which with me has constantly dominated all my good and all my evil qualities.' Yet at the same time there is a curious, haunting desire to love and to be loved, and an acknowledgment that genuine affection is one of the most worth-while things there is: 'In this world it is necessary to be loved in order to be happy.' Occasionally he made a friend, though he was apt to fight him before and afterwards. He really would have liked friends, would have liked simple, cordial intercourse with them, and there were moments when he tasted it, but for the most part again he did not have time.

Nor is the story much more profitable as regards relatives and family. Casanova's father is a mere shadow, and his mother is little more. He had to fight for himself from the beginning, and family affection meant little. He had brothers, one a distinguished painter, whom Jacques sometimes assisted and with whom he remained on very good terms. And this brother wrote to him with what sounds like genuine regard: 'If I were to lose you, no one in the world could fill the place in my heart that you now occupy.' There was also another brother, an abbé, even more disreputable than Jacques himself and whom consequently Jacques found peculiarly distasteful. Still, when the distaste reaches such a pitch of unfraternal acrimony as the following, one cannot feel that the disposition to brotherly tenderness was very deep-rooted: 'I should have seen him hanged with perfect indifference, not to say very great pleasure. Everybody has his morality, everybody his passions, and my favorite passion has always been vengeance.'

This isolation, this inherent individualism and restless independence of Casanova's is very marked in his attitude toward marriage. Occasionally some pretty woman gets hold of him and he thinks of the married state, when he cannot get her any other way. Even, as the years pile up, quiet and a home appear to have a certain charm—in imagination: 'I am persuaded I should have sacrificed everything for the happiness of a woman who deserved it.' But then did any woman deserve it? And when the yoke was just about to settle on his shoulders, he somehow slipped out from under. Manon Baletti, Esther d'O., Pauline — they were all very well, but liberty was better: 'I have loved women to madness, but I have always loved liberty even better, and when I found there was danger of losing it, I got out by hook or by crook.'

Nor was he any more enthusiastic about legitimate children than about a wife. He anticipates the chuckle of Dumas *père* over the three hundred children that he had scattered around the world: 'I laughed to myself to find my sons planted all over Europe.' When he meets a daughter, if she is pretty, he is interested, but the sons are apt to be a nuisance. Of one of them he says, 'As his heart seemed incapable of any generous impression, the little wretch was destined never to know friendship and never to have a friend' — not wholly unlike his father, it would appear. Curiously enough, one of the few cases in which Fanny Burney drops her syrupy graciousness is in the bitter analysis of her own only son.

So in general with regard to human relations it may be said of Casanova, as of Cæsar Borgia, that he stands alone, with the whole universe concentrated in himself — an attitude which might be fine, if any human being really could stand alone, without leaning — or trampling — upon someone else.

IV

It is obvious that such a life as Casanova's could not be lived without money, a good deal of it, and Casanova had very little in any assured form. He was born poor and he never had any really reliable source of income. Certainly it may be said that he never earned an honest dollar in his life, unless the few pennies that came from playing the 'cello in Venice. Nor did he ever show the slightest desire to accumulate wealth for itself. His thoughts were on other satisfactions, more tangible and more immediate.

At the same time, he always, or almost always, seemed to have money to spend when he wanted it. There were hard times and tight corners, when he bewailed the miseries of poverty and even thought suicide might be preferable. Then the dollars began to turn up again, somehow, and he used them, and enjoyed them. He liked fine clothes, fine food, fine equipages, needless to say fine women, and usually he had them.

He was generous, also, undeniably. When he wanted anything, he took it from anybody, but when anybody else wanted anything, he gave it, if he had it to give. He enlarges on his own merits in this line, as in all others: 'Benevolence has always had charms for me and I have never neglected to practice it upon occasion.' Perhaps the heartfelt acknowledgment of one of his beneficiaries may go a little further than his self-praise: 'I am confused in not knowing how to thank you for the kindness of heart which you show in remembering to help me in the very great need of money that overwhelms me.' That at least has a genuine ring.

When we look for the sources of Casanova's rather fleeting wealth, there seem to be three upon which he mainly relied. The first of these was the gaming-table. In a desperately gambling age, few were more rabid on the subject than Casanova. And he had the real gambler's spirit, would play at times till he lost everything and more: 'The hope of recovering what I had lost made me lose all I had.' That is the note again and again. But he had a long, shrewd head, knew how to choose his games and the people he played with. Nor did he hesitate a moment to take every advantage that could be reasonably, that is safely, taken. The delicate closeness to the wind with which he liked to sail appears in his remark: 'I was firmly resolved no longer to play as a dupe, but only when I had all the advantages which a prudent young man can provide for himself without leaving an opening for anyone to attack his honor.' And then, like so many others in an unbelieving age, he had a blind confidence in his luck, with all sorts of queer quips and quirks of belief in a friendly, favoring destiny which would somehow look out for him, if he let himself go. Either destiny, or his own ingenuity, or his impudence, or a combination of all three, seemed to arrange things somehow, so that he generally came out on top of the game. And again and again the veritable gambler's spirit peeps through: 'At that time I was playing mainly from pure avarice. I liked spending, and I regretted it when I was not spending money gained at play, for that alone I seemed to have picked up for nothing.'

Besides the cards and the dice, another source of income was the man's fertile and eager brain working in all forms of invention. At one time he set up a factory to develop a special process of silk-making and incidentally an industrial fortune. But with Casanova's natural proclivities the factory with its forty working girls soon became a harem, and the fortune vanished with a disastrous ease that would have disillusioned anyone else. For a time he was connected with the royal lottery in France, made a good income out of it, and would have made a better if those in authority would have listened to him. He tried to get back to Venice by offering commercial secrets which would have enriched his country — and himself. But the Venetian rulers cared little for his secrets, and less for him. He no sooner arrived in Spain than he laid before the prime minister a project for changing that arid country into a mine of agricultural wealth. But the minister was cold, perhaps the project was a little airy, and there was always a pretty girl waiting around the corner, who was better than any pro-

ject. After a night with her, you had not much
energy for projects or anything else.

But the most reliable financial resource of all
was the dupes. Menon, according to Xenophon,
believed that to cheat your enemies was waste of
time, because they were on their guard, but it was
the part of a wise man to cheat such an easy mark
as your friends. Casanova might have balked at
the bare theory, but his practice a good deal
savored of it. It was an age of charlatanism, and
people who believed in nothing else were ready
to accept every sort of magical chicanery. Such
jugglers as Cagliostro and Saint-Germain made
princely fortunes. Casanova's elderly friend and
patron in Venice, Bragadin, was much inclined to
occult practices and did all he could to develop the
taste in his young acquaintance. At first Casanova
was utterly scornful. But, after all, why not? If
you believed in nothing, anything might be true.
The Cabbala might have mystical secrets, there
might be strange power in numerical calculations,
human destiny might as well be written in the stars
as anywhere else. If they could keep Casanova's
yawning pockets well filled, surely they could do
anything. It is delightful to hear him pour out
apologies, when even his conscience occasionally
pricks him. These people were begging to be duped.
Someone would do it if he did not, and who could
do it more gently? 'You need not quarrel with
me when you see me emptying the purses of my
friends to furnish my caprices, for these friends had

chimerical projects and when I made them look for success in such, I was simply endeavoring to cure them by disabusing them.'

So the good-natured Bragadin was played upon to supply an income as long as he lived. And the delicious Esther d'O. in Holland was taken on as a pupil, till even Casanova's hardened compunction rebelled, and he tried to explain to her — only to find that she absolutely refused to believe him. And, best, or worst, of all, the Marquise d'Urfé in Paris, an elderly woman who was mad to get back youth and looks and love by magic or in any other way, took him to her heart. For years, until her death, he played upon her and preyed upon her with every device and trick of charlatanry. Truly, he might have adopted as his the motto which Talleyrand cynically proclaimed a few years later: 'Society is divided into two classes, the shearers and the shorn: one should always be with the first as against the second.'

v

But back of the money, back of the women, back of everything was always that incurable instinct of roving, of adventure, of vagabondage, for it is strange to trace this common element in Casanova and Saint Francis, when in other respects they were as far apart as the poles. Always to be moving, changing, seeing new faces, thinking new thoughts, penetrating into new worlds. The man's very name is full of suggestion, Casanova — New

House — a different abode and different surroundings every day. And again one is reminded of the verses of Donne which I quoted in connection with Francis,

> Be thou thine own home and in thyself dwell;
> Inn anywhere; continuance maketh hell.

Assuredly continuance was hell to Casanova, something different he would have, even if it was sometimes hateful, and in the search for such difference he ran into a list of adventures strange and perilous as those of Saint Paul. Saint Paul, to be sure, was serving Christ. Casanova was also devoutly serving J. C., but except for the initials there was little resemblance.

There is no doubt that Casanova would have liked larger political adventure, felt that he distinctly had it in him to become a Mazarin or a Disraeli. Perhaps he had, but somehow circumstances never favored its coming out. It seems much more probable, however, that he was merely one of the dreamers and that decisive, aggressive action would hardly have befitted him in such a broader sphere. Anyway, he had that fatal primary preoccupation always getting between his feet and tripping him up, in political ambition as well as in literary. Cæsar, Cæsar Borgia, Napoleon, liked women well enough, but no more than the writers would they have let a woman interfere with their future for a moment. Casanova, like Aaron Burr, found it more amusing to trifle with a fleeting toy than to labor long hours for a dubious hope. Consequently, his adventures, exciting and exhausting as they were, were all personal and domestic, and in many cases trivial and sordid, descending sometimes even to futile practical jokes, which resulted in one case in permanently incapacitating the victim. 'I was sorry,' says Casanova, characteristically, 'but as I had not the slightest intention of hurting him, and as I considered that the trick he had before played me might have cost my life, I was very quickly consoled.'

In such a life as this it was clearly necessary to have your hand on your sword and to know how to use it. Casanova was no bravo, always looking for a fight: 'I have never feared to cross swords with the first comer, but I have never cared for the barbaric pleasure of shedding man's blood.' Moreover, he had an almost morbid dread of death, perhaps natural in one so intensely alive. But when you are taking love or cash from every quarter, you have to be prepared to protect yourself. So there were battles everywhere, sometimes quick and sudden rencontres, sometimes elaborate and formal duels, carried on with all possible dignity and propriety. The best known of these is the meeting with the Polish nobleman Branicki, described both in the *Mémoires* and in a long and detailed separate narrative. Needless to say, that Casanova, according to his own account, behaved well, and luckily there are reports of others which fairly bear him out.

CARL A. RUDISILL LIBRARY
LENOIR RHYNE COLLEGE

Also, there were endless hairbreadth escapes from perilous situations, escapes which lose nothing in the telling, as is certainly true of the complicated breaking away after months of confinement in the deadly prisons of the leads or roofs at Venice. Casanova gives a hair-raising detail, again both in the *Mémoires* and in a separate document, of this surprising adventure, the wild, final clambering over gutters and chimneys to ever-vanishing safety. Unfortunately, one of Casanova's admirers, M. Guède, has tested the narrative by a careful study of the situation and declares the details to be utterly false, and necessarily so. But this is not at all surprising, for in all of Casanova the false and the true are so inextricably blended that it would not be possible to disentangle them, if it were worth while to try.

After years of this sort of thing, with all its dangers and discomforts, it was not unnatural that even an inveterate vagabond should have his moments of longing for home and peace and quiet. In 1772 he writes to Baron Bavois: 'For two years now I have been tormented with the Swiss malady, *Heimweh* [homesickness], and I verily believe that I shall die of it.' When he actually got back to Venice, home seemed — for a little while — singularly delightful. The strange thing was that nobody took any notice of him, he might just as well have been dead. This would not do at all. The front stage had always been his place, the front stage he must have, and so the roving restlessness overcame

him again and never forsook him as long as his
ageing limbs would respond to it. One vivid passage indicates the undying dreams, the never-failing
visions of possibility that always lured him on:
'I still believe even today that when a man gets it
into his head to realize a certain project, no matter
what, and occupies himself only with that, he is
bound to accomplish it, no matter what the difficulties: such a man may become Grand Visier, he
may become Pope, he may overthrow a monarchy,
provided he starts early enough; for a man who has
reached the age despised by Fortune will accomplish nothing and without her aid there is no use in
hoping for success. You must count upon her and
at the same time despise her reverses, but it is a
very difficult calculation.' Which may perhaps be
called the gambler's and adventurer's creed. Note
that he does not specify the age, and probably he
never felt that it had come for him.

VI

The *Mémoires* of Casanova close with the year
1774, though they were written twenty years later
and he proposed to fill up the gap. In 1774 he
managed his restoration to Venice, hoping that he
was going to play a considerable public part there.
But the best employment he could obtain was one
for which he was admirably fitted, that of a police
spy, perhaps we should say a stool-pigeon, in the
service of the Venetian Inquisitorial Commissioners. He served here for a while and wrote eminently

edifying reports on public morals, which are still
preserved in the archives. But even he felt somewhat humiliated, and the roving habit got hold of
him again for another ten years.

Then in 1785 he was invited by Count Waldstein, who had taken a fancy to his showy and
varied and especially his magical erudition, to become librarian in Waldstein's solitary castle of
Dux, in the lonely forests of Bohemia. Casanova
accepted, but afterwards admitted that it was a mistake, on Waldstein's part, and still more on his own.
The bitterness he came to feel is very manifest in
one almost tragic passage: 'They say that this
Dux is a delightful spot, and I see that it might be
for many; but not for me, for what delights me in
my old age is independent of the place which I in-
habit. When I do not sleep, I dream, and when I
am tired of dreaming, I blacken paper, then I read,
and most often reject all that my pen has vomited.'

When the master of the house was at home,
it was not so bad: then there was a certain kind
of society. But often he was absent, and the servants were indifferent, impudent, and neglectful.
Casanova, in his fretted weariness, quarreled with
them, and more often quarreled with himself. He
was old, worn down by fatigue and disease, he was
dependent, he was poor; worst of all, he was lonely,
ghastly lonely, he who had always had the clash of
other souls and bodies to make life interesting.
The loneliness is even so bitter that it drives him
to regretting marriage and the domestic affection

which he had often scorned: 'With my character perhaps I did well not to attach myself irrevocably, though at my age my very independence becomes a sort of slavery. If I had married a woman clever enough to have managed me, to have dominated me, without my being aware of the domination, I should have looked out for my fortune, I should have had children by her, and I should not be as I am now, alone in the world without anything whatever.'

In these long, barren, and tedious years the one refuge and resource was memory, and Casanova delighted to call up before his fancy those scores of lovely faces, gay or gracious, merry or tender, mocking or alluring, and to disentangle all the sunny threads of association that were entwined with them. But if he enjoyed it, perhaps others would too, might be amused even if they were not edified. And he sets to work to write his *Mémoires* with the same ardor which he threw into everything: 'I write thirteen hours a day, which pass as if they were thirteen minutes.' To be sure, the said *Mémoires* strike even him as queer things at times: 'The story of my Life will be a work the reading of which will be forbidden in every country where morals are respected.' Perhaps it would be better to burn it, but he never does, and he knows he never would.

It is interesting to note that there is very little of remorse or compunction in the later Casanova any more than in the earlier. Occasionally such things may suggest themselves, but he waves them away. It all comes back to the old apology: I was born with these mad instincts and capacities for pleasure, why should I not develop and indulge them in every way I can? To be sure, even Casanova hardly attains the self-assurance of Dumas *père's* gorgeous declaration: 'When the hand of the Lord closes the two horizons of my life, letting fall the veil of his love between the nothingness that precedes and the nothingness that follows the life of man, he may examine the intermediate space with his most rigorous scrutiny, he will not find there one single evil thought or one action for which I feel that I should reproach myself.' But if Casanova would not have said it, I do not think he would have minded having some of his fervent admirers say it.

No, the prevailing note of these dismal years is not remorse but regret, bitter longing to recall the past, and to live it over again and a lot more of the same kind. To live just his own life over, as he had lived it, would be indeed delightful, but he would be willing to sink even lower to avoid that horrible death: 'To have the splendid privilege of being born again, I would consent not only to be a woman, but to be a brute, of any sort whatever.' How different from many of us, who do not know of any life in the whole wide world that we should like to live over, least of all our own, and certainly not Jacques Casanova's!

Then into this atmosphere of arid desolation

came the delightful episode of Cécile de Roggendorff, the last of Casanova's innumerable loves.
And here at least we are assured that there was
no sexual taint by the only guarantee which would
serve with Casanova even at seventy, the fact that
the parties never met and that their acquaintance
was wholly epistolary.

Mademoiselle de Roggendorff was a young lady
of a noble Austrian family but poor, and her relatives were anxious to keep her out of the way as
much as possible. Driven to despair by solitude
and privation, she learned that the great Casanova
was living at Dux, and that he was an intimate
friend of her brother, and she decided to appeal
to him for advice and sympathy. Fortunately, a
number of her letters are preserved among the Dux
manuscripts, and they are most attractive in their
eager hero-worship, even with all their candid delusion as to Casanova himself. She begs him not
only to advise her, but to lecture her: 'Show me my
errors, if you blame my principles; the esteem I feel
for you will lead me to change them.' Gradually he
becomes her ideal, almost her idol, and she enlarges
ecstatically on 'the confidence which I feel renewed
in me when I read your lines, what purity of
morals I discover in them, what justness of principle, what delicacy of feeling, a delicacy that simply
enchants me!'

And after the first gasp of astonishment, Casanova
rises gallantly to the opportunity. Unfortunately,
we have not his actual letters, but simply Cécile's

quotations from them, which are exhilarating enough: 'True love is that to which sensual enjoyment is unknown.' And he writes to Cécile's brother, who not unnaturally expressed some anxiety as to too close a connection: 'I have instilled into her the love of truth, moderation, submission, a noble pride which in no way resembles haughtiness, and in short all the virtues made for her sex and analogous to the sense of honor in man.'

Rank and disgusting hypocrisy! the reader will cry. But it was not deliberate hypocrisy at all. Casanova had always prized virtue — at a distance. Like Milton's Satan, he saw

> Virtue in her shape how lovely, saw and pined
> Her loss.

It was simply that he had not had much acquaintance with her. Take a most striking comparison, that of Sainte-Beuve. Sainte-Beuve was as wild a frequenter of woman as Casanova was, perhaps in earlier years more sentimental, but when he grew old and busy, he contented himself with a street-corner promiscuity which even Casanova would have despised. As he murmured to Goncourt: 'One should make the tour of everything and believe in nothing: there is nothing real but woman.' And elsewhere, 'My ideal is fine hair, fine teeth, fine shoulders, and the rest: I am quite indifferent to dirt.' Yet during this very same period Sainte-Beuve was writing the twenty-eight volumes of *Lundis*, with the most delicate, sympathetic, understanding analysis of all the finer virtues of woman that has ever been made by man, as in the Eugénie de Guérin. There was no hypocrisy. We are simply seeing differing facets of that marvelously complicated spirit. Take a more vividly concentrated case, that of Aaron Burr. Burr adored women in the same way as Casanova and Sainte-Beuve. All his life he indulged his passions and followed his whims, without the faintest regard to order or propriety. Yet as Vice-President he could proclaim solemnly to the Senate of the United States: 'On full investigation it will be discovered that there is scarce a departure from order but leads to or is indissolubly connected with a departure from morality.' Once more, there is no deliberate hypocrisy. Burr had the highest esteem for order and morality both, but he had never happened to have much to do with either of them.

Hypocrisy or no hypocrisy, the sweet, sunny, gracious idyl of Cécile de Roggendorff forms a charming epilogue to this lifelong orgy of mad riot and licentious debauch.

IV
ALONE WITH GOD
THOMAS À KEMPIS

CHRONOLOGY

THOMAS HAMMERKEN.
  Born, Kempen, May, 1380(?).
  At school at Deventer, 1392.
  Entered Convent of Mount Saint Agnes, 1399(?).
  Took orders, 1413.
  Imitation written, 1415–1420(?).
  Became Sub-Prior, 1425.
  Convent closed, 1429–1432.
  Again Sub-Prior, 1447.
  Died, July 26, 1471.

THOMAS À KEMPIS AND THE MONASTERY OF MOUNT ST. AGNES

IV

ALONE WITH GOD
THOMAS À KEMPIS

I

'CONSIDER that God and you are alone in the universe, and you will have great peace in your heart.' That is the dominant note of the *Imitation of Christ* and of its reputed author, Thomas à Kempis. The outer world is of no consequence whatever, and all our thought, all our effort, all our love, should be concentrated upon the inner. The fragile, glittering splendor of the outer world is fading, elusive, and transitory, unless you can find some enduring reality beneath it. The author of the *Imitation* found this reality in God, and all his life was concerned with nothing else: 'Consider that God and you are alone in the universe, and you will have great peace in your heart.'

Thomas Hammerken was born at Kempen, near Cologne, about 1380. His father, John, a worker in metal, and his mother, Gertrude, trained him piously, and so far as any record goes he might have grown up for the Church from his infancy. He had a good elementary education, and, when he was thirteen years old, he went to a religious community at Deventer, called The Congregation of Common Life, established by Florentius Rade-

wyn under the guidance of Gerard Groot and af-
filiated with the Augustinian Order. Here he remained seven years and then was admitted to the
Monastery of Saint Agnes, at Zwolle, where he
took orders in 1413. The remainder of Thomas's
long life, till he died at over ninety, in 1471, was
passed in monastic retirement. The *Imitation* was
written probably between 1415 and 1420. In 1425,
Thomas was elected for a term Sub-Prior, and in
later life he again filled the same office. The most
violent commotion in his career was the closing of
the monastery by the ecclesiastical authorities for
a short period from 1429 to 1432. Except for this,
his days appear to have flowed on, one like another,
to the end. He was always busy, he was always
supremely occupied with God: 'There is nothing
great, there is nothing precious or admirable, there
is nothing worthy of repute; there is nothing lofty,
there is nothing praiseworthy or fit to be desired,
except what is eternal.'

Evidently to understand à Kempis we have to
see him in the background of the monastic life, for
he apparently knew little about any other, at any
rate by direct and immediate contact. And it
must be appreciated at once how infinitely remote
that life is from the bustle and the open air and the
universal publicity of the journalized and auto-
mobiled and radioed American world in which we
live today. We do not need the monastic life, as
the Middle Ages so often did, for a refuge from the
tumult and fierce struggle or barbarous passion

all about us, and its silence, its monotony, its austere remoteness, often make us shudder with disgust. Such a life absolutely required God and heaven — and perhaps also hell — to make it tolerable, and to many people today God and heaven, not to speak of hell, seem more remote even than the monasteries.

Human nature being what it is, it is obvious that even in the Middle Ages, while there were some to whom the monastic life was suited, there were many more to whom it was not. Some were forced into it by the pride and poverty of their families, some drifted into it almost by accident, some, perhaps the most tragic, entered it with furious, lofty fervor, only to find too late that it did not suit them at all, and to fret and pine away in futile regret. À Kempis himself gives a vivid picture of such misfits as they too often appeared at the divine services: 'And they gravely offend God, by rising indolently in the morning, by often coming to the service late, by singing listlessly, by slurring the words, by turning uneasily, by gazing around them idly, by listening inattentively, by bowing irreverently, by yawning over the length of the psalms, and by manifestly hurrying through to the end.' For the mass of mankind grow weary with too much solemnity and austerity, but these people were tied to such things by an oath they could never break.

It is frequently charged also that the monastic life bred idleness. In a sense this charge is unjust.

All the great monastic leaders emphasized the necessity of occupation, of constant, useful work. À Kempis himself says: 'By labor mischievous leisure is avoided and the frivolous chatter too often engendered by leisure.... He will always be richer in goodness who has been a faithful worker.'

No, the monks were not idle, but their labor was in danger of degenerating into a monotonous routine, which filled the hands but not the head. In some temperaments no doubt this fostered a dreamy sweet serenity, as appears in the study of the monk Sirenius:

> In quiet cell my quiet hours I spend,
>   A round of daily duties daily done,
>   Now slipping through my fingers, one by one,
> My well-worn beads, which well-worn prayers attend,
> Now adding gorgeous tints to what I penned
>   About the Holy Mary and her Son:
>   The task, so long, so long ago begun,
> Goes leisurely, I would not have it end.
> They say there's wild work in the world outside,
> Princes and kings are hurrying far and wide,
>   There's crowns set on awry, crowns rent away.
> And sometimes, in vague murmurs from afar,
> I hear the crash and din of hideous war:
>   What care I, so they let me paint and pray?

But many others were restless, riotous, rebellious, and while the stories of conventual vice and disorder may have been overdrawn, they were prevalent enough to make a serious blot on the picture. Nor did the reluctance of the Church to admit these things help matters greatly, though, as the historian says, 'Much as the Church hated sin, it hated scandal even more.'

Perhaps even more insidious and dangerous than the actual vice was the conventual melancholy, the dreaded *accidia*, which, when it fairly seized a monk, seldom let him go, and made him unfit for this world or the other: 'If *accidia* once laid hold upon a monk he was lost; ceasing to perform with active mind his religious duties, he would find them a meaningless, endless routine, filling him with irritation, with boredom, and with a melancholy against which he might struggle in vain.' To which there must be added the evils which beset institutional life everywhere and at all times, the friction, the jealousy, the backbiting and scandal, which affect the human spirit when it is crowded into an abnormal and excessive contact with others. Someone speaks of 'the undercurrent of hate which prevails in every boarding-house,' and such an undercurrent will manifest itself wherever human beings are herded too closely.

Perhaps the gravest charge of all that can be brought against the monastic life is that of selfishness, and this charge has frequently been advanced by Protestant critics against even the *Imitation*. The monk is preoccupied with his own soul and leaves the vast rest of the world to take care of itself. It is impossible to deny a certain truth in this, even as regards Thomas à Kempis. At the same time, it should be remembered that the theoretical ideal of the monastic life, so far from being selfish, was the complete abnegation and destruction of self and the setting an example to the whole world of this very thing. Moreover, the cry of selfishness often comes from those who, under the pretense of active philanthropy, are busily engaged in the violent, aggressive, dominating assertion of self, who, while they profess and perhaps believe that they are giving their lives to the service of others, are really using others in great part for their own glory. So subtle and so complicated is the cunning intrusion of self into every shred and thread of our obscure and too easily deluded souls.

The real secret and excuse and value of the monastic life, when it worked, undoubtedly lay in the search for and the possession of God, and the infinite peace that such possession brought with it. A suggestion of that peace appears in an account of the Convent of the Grande Chartreuse: 'The common world has no idea of such peace, it is a different earth from ours, a changed human nature. You feel it, you cannot define it, this peace which grows upon you. I have seen the laughter of a child's simplicity on the lips of old age, and gravity and a sweet solemnity of spirit in the features of youth.' It is the peace of God which passeth all understanding.

Whatever defects the monastic career might develop in others, it would seem that the long, simple life of Thomas à Kempis went far to realize what was best in it. His picture of the ideal monk appears to fit himself, though he certainly did not mean it so: 'He issues forth rarely, he lives apart, he eats sparingly, he dresses poorly, he labors much, he speaks little, watches long, rises early, prays assiduously, reads constantly, and in everything he keeps the rule from pure love of it.' There are hints and intimations that there was a passionate, ardent human soul under all the regularity, but for seventy years that soul was disciplined and accorded to the will of God.

It was a simple life, a gentle life, a sincere life, and it would be cruel indeed to call it a selfish one. During all the years of it the man worked. He was a copyist, a profession which was serious before the invention of printing. He copied the whole Bible from beginning to end, and he copied endless other works. Also he did a great amount of original writing of his own, seven solid volumes of mediæval Latin. Whether his life was selfish or not, it was certainly not unoccupied.

The question arises whether the *Imitation of Christ* may rightly be included among these works of à Kempis. There has been an unceasing controversy on the subject and the controversy shows no signs of coming to an end. But on the whole the solid scholarship of Hirsche and others would seem to throw the balance in favor of Thomas, and none of the other suggested authors has anything like such a substantial claim. The mere apparent superiority of the *Imitation* to à Kempis's other

writings would not seem to mean more than the
superiority of the *Elegy* or *Don Quixote* to the other
writings of Gray and Cervantes. And an exten-
sive perusal of the seven Latin volumes makes this
superiority in à Kempis's case seem much less
than is often asserted. At the same time there is no
disputing that the *Imitation* is the distilled quin-
tessence of à Kempis's life and work, if he really
wrote it, and its enormous popularity in all languages and with all sorts of readers, profane as well
as religious, makes it the supreme manual of the
religious life and of the subdual of the human soul
to the God who made it.

II

To begin with, there is the simple, direct, general
subdual of self, the overcoming, the putting down,
the eliminating of that turbulent impulse to assert and maintain one's own ego which necessarily
means the suppression, the injury, the limiting of
others. As à Kempis puts it, 'Know that the love
of yourself harms you more than anything else in
the whole world.' The foundation, the root, of
this love of self is the desire of things, that fatal
wanting which Saint Francis all his life proclaimed
to be so deadly, and à Kempis, like Saint Francis,
insists that desire must be rooted out altogether if
perfection is to be attained. Desire is not only
selfish in conception and cruel in execution, but it
never brings contentment, and instead only unhap-
piness and restlessness: 'Whenever a man desires

anything inordinately, he at once becomes disquieted.'

It is true that à Kempis, with his penetrating insight, knew well that self would find a way to insinuate its fatal poison into even the effort to get rid of self. There are many who take pride, unconsciously perhaps, on their success in sacrifice, in humility, in abnegation. But that does not shake his steady aim and purpose, for himself and for others, to crush and to eliminate the deadly tendency to get and not to give.

The summing up, the acme, the concentrated essence of self is in the conception of sin, and it is the apparently complete disappearance of that conception at the present day that makes it so difficult for us to enter into much of à Kempis's attitude. It is this brooding horror of sin, which perhaps after all had its spiritual advantages, that explains Pascal's bitter cry: 'The true and unique virtue is to hate one's self.' Self in this sense means sin. Sin is always busy with the pleasures of this life, and à Kempis and the *Imitation* wage eternal war upon these pleasures, as being transitory, delusive, and in the end full of bitterness and disgust. 'Oh, what a comforting conscience would he have who never pursued the joys which fade, who never occupied himself with the fleeting pleasures of this world!' And it must be remembered that the substantial background to these trivial enjoyments which vanish away is the sure and solid permanence of the heavenly reward for those who

eschew the others and in à Kempis's equal conviction the solid permanence of hell. Keep these
things before you, the secure eternal splendor of the
redeemed saints and the fathomless misery of the
sinners who have gone astray, and you will find the
constant warfare easy. But it is constant and in
this world it is never ending, for the pleasures of
the day appear for the day unutterably sweet, and
the soul of man is mobile and readily diverted
from what is remote, though everlasting: 'The
whole man flows away to external things, and unless
he quickly gets a hold upon himself, he is dissolved
in all that floats about him.'

As the author of the *Imitation* battles with desire
in general, so he over and over analyzes and
specifies the varied details and aspects of it, and
brands and lashes them with his simple, unescap-
able condemnation. There is riches. Brought up
as à Kempis had been, in the conventual, community life, in which personal possessions played no
part, it might seem as if he could know nothing
about riches. But here, as elsewhere, he shows a
strange comprehension of the larger movement of
the outside world. Riches and possessions burden
and weary even those who seem to grasp them most
securely. They distract not only from your eternal
welfare, but from the ease and serenity of life led
here: 'The more a man gathers things to himself,
the more he is hampered and distracted.' Riches
corrupt those who have them and those who have
them not, for those who have want more and those

who have not want what the others have. They corrupt even the saints, who are unconsciously led to flatter and bow down and have to be cautioned most earnestly: 'Do not flatter the wealthy, and be not eager to show yourself among the magnates of the world.' The whole attitude towards possessions is made plain, as so often, in one perfect sentence: 'Give up all things, and you shall find all things; give up desire, and you shall find repose.'

Take another almost equally general and equally insidious aspect of worldly interest, the love of reputation and flattery and applause. Again à Kempis understands perfectly how universal this is, how it affects not only the sinners but the saints, with its thousand creeping, insinuating manifestations. Glory allures and enchants us all, not only the glory of sin and selfishness, but the glory of good works and useful achievements. As the Eastern sage has it, 'All other vanities are curable, but the vanity of a saint can never be rooted out.' À Kempis, living all his life in quiet shadow, avoiding honors, avoiding dignities, even such minor ones as were offered him, preaches everywhere the vanity of worldly honor and the futility of wordly praise: 'Fly praise as if it were poison.... Vain and foolish are those who delight in the commendations of men.' And the grand words of the *Imitation* sum it up even more impressively: 'The cheat deceives the cheat, the vain the vain, the blind the blind, the weak the weak, whilst they extol them, and in truth one rather puts another to confusion whilst he vainly praises him.'

As praise and glory are to be despised and rejected, so also is the vain pursuit of knowledge. It is evident that à Kempis himself was no wide or persistent scholar; both the *Imitation* and his other works make this clear enough. He was a most assiduous reader of the Bible. Biblical allusions and turns and suggestions appear in all his writings constantly. Also there is more or less knowledge of the mystics and generally devotional writers who had preceded him. But wordly learning and the love of study for itself get little favor. He knows the charm of them. With all those quiet hours of thought and reflection, such a temperament could not be unaware of the charm of books of all sorts or any sort. He recognizes the occasional profit of such studies and the legitimacy of them when kept in proper limits: 'Science is not to be found fault with, nor the simple knowledge of things as they are, which is good considered in itself, and is ordained of God; but these are of much less consequence than a good conscience and a virtuous life!'

The trouble with worldly learning is that it puffs a man up, exalts his opinion of his own gifts and powers, and destroys humility. The saying of Aristotle is all very well, à Kempis thinks. 'Every man naturally desires to know; but what is knowledge worth if it does not carry with it the fear of God?' And he urges and enjoins a persistent caution in such matters: 'Abstain from the excessive desire of knowing; for it carries much distraction with it, and much deception. Men wish to seem learned and to be called wise. There are many things which when they are known bring little or no profit to the soul.'

The quiet monk, sitting in his quiet cell, with the wisdom of God to enlighten him, knew enough of human learning to understand full well that the largest reach of it is but a faint spark, quivering for an instant in the fathomless darkness of ignorance. If this was true in à Kempis's day, five hundred years ago, how much truer is it now, when the range of man's possible knowledge has increased so vastly more than his capacity to grasp it. May we not say with even more conviction than à Kempis did, 'The science of all sciences is to know that we know nothing'?

Nor is this firm and consistent God-lover any more tolerant of beauty than he is of knowledge. There is not one gleam of the arts and their passionate seduction in all his writing. Are not the arts, one and all of them, intimately bound up with human passion and human sin? Is not their witchery too nearly related to unholy impulses of indulgence or despair? Painting, to be sure, may illustrate sacred themes, but danger is always perilously inherent in it. At any rate, the quiet monk feels a good deal safer without it. Music is and always has been a prominent element of worship. As such you must accept it and even participate in it. But the rapture of music is for God and not for you. To you it is merely the performance of a religious duty.

Even the love of the exquisite outdoor world, which seems so simple and innocent, is at least distracting. À Kempis cherishes nothing of the charming vagabondage of Saint Francis. The birds and the fishes may be our brothers, but let them pursue their own salvation as their instincts guide them. And he condemns idle strolling, which may lure the eyes so far out of the way: 'The inclinations of sensuality lead you to walk abroad, but when the hour is past, what do you bring back but a burdened conscience and a scattered heart? A joyous setting forth often brings a sad returning home, and a gay evening may be the prelude to a melancholy morning.... What can you see anywhere that you do not see here? Here is the sky, and the earth, and all the elements, and of these are all things made. ... Leave vain things to the vain, and do you attend to those things which God has prescribed for you.'

So in everything there is the urgent, ardent injunction to avoid mere curiosity, the flitting and fluttering of soul in external details which divert and distract it from the weightier business that should be its whole vital concern. There were no Sunday papers in the Monastery of Mount Saint Agnes, and it is easy to imagine what à Kempis would have thought of them. 'Leave all curiosity behind you.' It would not be the motto for a Sunday paper.

THOMAS À KEMPIS

It goes without saying that the grosser forms of desire are not to be tolerated for a moment in this scheme of things. The body must be nourished and cherished after a fashion, while we have it, more's the pity, but let us deplore the necessity, not encourage it or foster it: 'Oh, if we never needed to eat, or drink, or sleep, but could praise God all the time and give ourselves only to spiritual studies!' It is to be feared that this program would not altogether commend itself in modern educational institutions. But à Kempis gives his view of the matter with his usual marvelous precision and point: '*Sint temporalia in usu, aeterna in desiderio*, Use the temporal, desire the eternal.'

It should be said, however, that, with these principles of extreme apparent austerity, à Kempis, naturally gentle and kindly, does not seem disposed to insist upon the harsher methods of self-discipline which were so often resorted to in the desperate effort to make the spirit overcome the flesh. He does occasionally refer to such things, but his emphasis and his insistence are rather upon spiritual pressure, the urgency and agency of prayer and meditation upon those higher, more eternal themes which make the temptations and distractions of this world seem insignificant. 'The flesh will murmur,' he says, 'but it may be restrained by the fervor of the spirit.' The refuge, the protection, the sure guide and help, is to be found in the sense of the splendor, and the glory, and the eternity of those who belong to God: 'The desire of the flesh, the lust of the eye, and the pride of life draw us to the love of this world, but the grief and misery that justly follow these things bring loathing and weariness of the world ... and he who pursues them sees not and tastes not the sweetness of God and the inward excellence of virtue.'

III

So far the direct subdual of self in immediate wants and desires. But there is further the subdual of self with reference to other human beings. À Kempis here insists constantly upon the habit of solitude, upon the love of your own cell and abiding place, not merely the rule of it, but the love of it. And of course it is not your cell for yourself, but for the presence of God in it, with the incessant reiteration of the reminder: 'Consider that God and you are alone in the universe, and you will have great peace in your heart.'

Naturally this does not mean that duty to others should be neglected. There should be consideration, there should be courtesy, there should be thoughtfulness, always. You have your duty to others and you should see that it is done. But the duty to God comes first and is more satisfying in its fulfillment. It is true that solitude, merely as such, has its dangers. In the quaint phrase of old Burton, who knew so much about it, 'solitude is the shoeing-horn of melancholy.' An unoccupied, a mischievous solitude, may bring about the *accidia*, not to speak of other evils of all sorts. Solitude is only complete and perfect and ideal when it is filled with God. Again, there is a restless and perturbed solitude, solitude that is sought from duty and not because one loves it. In this matter habit is everything. When you are filled with the twentieth-century American habit of motion, of feeling that you must be forever on the go, always seeing and hearing and doing some new thing, solitude becomes irksome and distasteful. To settle down to quiet is the one thing you hate, and mere physical quiet is nothing without spiritual peace. The habit of solitude, the habit of quiet, the habit of peace, grows upon you like other habits, and this has never been better expressed than in à Kempis's lovely words, '*Cella continuata dulcescit, et male custodita taedium generat*, Thy cell, if thou continue in it, grows sweet; but, if thou keep not to it, it becomes wearisome.'

Certainly it would appear that no one could have cultivated the cell habit much more strictly all his life than did à Kempis. Indeed this solitude has led some lovers of the *Imitation* to dispute his authorship of the book. Every page of it seems to indicate a profound, searching knowledge of the human heart in all its depth and intricacy, which could hardly have been acquired within the walls of a conventual prison. In answer to which we may perhaps suggest the remark of Sénancour, 'If I have not experienced everything, I have at least imagined everything.' Imagination and sensibility, as we can see clearly that à Kempis possessed them, enable a man to divine the secrets of the world's soul in the secrets of his own. At any rate, no one has ever preached the charm of solitude — with God — more insistently and more persuasively than the author of the *Imitation*: 'To leave your cell is always perilous, and to dwell quietly within it is the peaceful haven of a religious life.'

The chief temptation with regard to others is the desire to rule and control them, and in dominating spirits this desire may assert itself as vehemently in the cloister as in the palace. The saint and the servant of God is quite as apt to seek the leadership of others, always for their good of course, as the soldier or the statesman. To à Kempis himself this form of temptation seems to have made little appeal. He was obviously of the very unruling class, who shun responsibility more than anything else in the world, who would get rid of it even for themselves if they could, and would on no account undertake it for others. Help others, serve others, minister to others, as far as you can, he urges, but leave the control of others to those who care for it, and let them remember that there is danger to themselves and to others also in every step they take.

Another form of the relation to others which requires the utmost watchfulness is temper, wrath, anger, whether justified or not. Here again, à Kempis would seem to have had himself a gentle and quiet disposition to which such stormy outbursts would have been peculiarly foreign. Yet under the calm aspect there is sometimes more furious tumult than appears, and more effort is needed to secure and maintain the calm than would go into a tempestuous victory: 'There are those,' says the *Imitation*, 'who keep themselves in peace and also have peace with others. And there are those who neither have peace themselves nor leave others in peace; such are a burden to others and always a still more grievous burden to themselves.' And elsewhere à Kempis indicates his judgment of quarrelers in no uncertain terms: 'When thou art proud or angry, when thou backbitest, murmurest, deceivest, liest, and disturbest others, rejoicest at their evil, and repinest at their good… then thou followest the Devil.' What more can be said?

But besides actual loud wrath and quarreling, there is the vague aversion and dislike, the distaste we form for our neighbors, often with no reasonable or even conscious ground, but which, if it is indulged, grows irritating and hateful, and often poisons our own lives more than theirs. Get rid of all such harmful instincts, tear them out, root them up, cries à Kempis. Do not dwell upon the faults, or defects, or weaknesses, of others, do not urge them or amplify them: 'You are not yet in heaven with the holy angels, but in the actual world, with men good and evil, and the evil will never be wanting in this region of the shadow of death.' The one sure cure for criticism and fault-finding is to remember that you yourself have probably just such defects and certainly plenty of others: 'For as your eye judges others, so in your turn will others judge

you.' Or, as it is put by the Orlando of Shakespeare,
who was in many ways so close to à Kempis, for all
the difference in their lives, 'I will chide no breather
in the world but myself, against whom I know most
faults.'

As animosity, bitterness, and hostility are to be
rooted out, so also is the idle curiosity which sometimes under the guise of kindly interest diverts its
own emptiness by prying and intruding into the
affairs and lives of others. There is always the excuse of being active and useful, but the activity too
often gets nowhere and the utility is apt to be
futility. 'Do you wrap yourself in the peace of
God, and let the agitator agitate as much as he
will.' A curious interest in the affairs of others is
only too apt to degenerate into gossip and scandal,
and at best you are wasting your heart on lower
things when it might be occupied with higher:
'What is more foolish than to seek the trivial and
reject the true? What is more perverse than to neglect God and attend to man? What is madder than
to watch the world and let heaven slip away from
you?' The unprofitable performances, the unac-
countable struggles and ambitions of men, why
should you vex yourself to note or study them?
You have your own business with God, and that is
far more than enough to fill the few and fading
years that are afforded to you here: 'He who is well
disposed and well ordered within does not trouble
himself over the extraordinary and perverse con-
tortions of men.'

The remedy, the sure refuge, which the author of the *Imitation* has to offer for all these temptations and misleading complications with others is silence. What we seek so desperately — and too well he knows it — is somehow to get out of, to escape from, ourselves: 'It is for this that we talk so widely and so freely, because by the exchange of words we seek to console one another, and to cheer our hearts when they are wearied by many thoughts.' Then we learn — though some of us never learn — that such effort for escape is vain, that we cannot get out of ourselves, do what we will, and that the wide waste of words is the most empty delusion of all. So we come to appreciate the blessing and the fruitfulness of silence. To keep still rarely injures anyone. We are so often damaged by what we say, so rarely by what we do not say. If we sit silent and let the world go by, we are at least safe as regards others, and we have the positive advantage of having time and fresh attention to give to the matters that concern our own souls: 'It is the part of prudence to keep silent in evil days, to turn our thoughts inward, and not to be troubled by the judgments of men.'

But, it will be said, though we should avoid strife with others and even vain chatter about them, we should at least seek their support and friendship and affection. These things are very well, à Kempis admits; friends and friendship are useful and allow of our being useful in our turn. They should be recognized and cultivated, within limits. But they are terribly distracting, and at best they are uncertain. There is only one friendship that is secure and eternal: 'Too much confidence should not be placed in fragile, mortal man, even when he is useful and beloved, nor should you be too much disappointed even when he turns about and betrays your expectation. Those who are with you today may be against you tomorrow: they change like the wind.'

This mistrust of human support extends even to the natural ties of blood and family: 'He who clings to the created falls with that which is prone to fall.' It is surprising how little light we get on à Kempis's own family relations. It is said that in early life his mother was much to him. Probably she was, but he never alludes to her or to the relation in general. His elder brother was of great assistance to him in his monastic career and in return Thomas tended John in his last illness with assiduous care and apparent affection. But on the whole even natural love must not be relied upon too much. 'When man reaches the point where he seeks consolation from nothing created, then first he begins to acquire the perfect relish of God.' And it should be remembered that à Kempis had the strong injunction and the example of Jesus to the same effect. Only, in this as in other things, one may be reluctant to let go the earthly love till one has a more secure hold upon the heavenly.

With this attitude towards earthly affection generally, it is hardly necessary to emphasize à Kempis's view of the love for woman. There are, indeed, vague touches here and there which intimate that he knew what the desires of the flesh might be. But he disposes of the subject concisely when he says, 'Nothing so soils and entangles the heart of man as an impure passion for any created thing'; and the monastic attitude was never better summed up than in the sentence, 'Be not familiar with any one woman, but commend all good women in general to God.'

What is most important to the author of the *Imitation* in this matter of relations to other human beings is, as with Saint Francis, the exquisite virtue of implicit obedience, where the law of God calls for it. It is not of the least consequence that you should command others, but it is of the utmost consequence that you should learn to obey without questioning. 'It is a great sign of wisdom not to be precipitate in action, nor to persist obstinately in your own purposes.' You should obey, not only for the immediate object, but for the mere benefit of the virtue in itself: 'Study to do the will of others, rather than your own.' The precept may seem a long way off from twentieth-century America, but perhaps it has its value, all the more for that reason.

And none knows better than à Kempis that the deeper root of obedience is humility. If you want to subdue yourself, the first principle is to have a poor opinion of yourself, not to display such an opinion, with a mere Uriah Heep hypocrisy, but really to understand the vast weakness and inadequacy and incompetence of human nature, as it may be found in others, but as you know, at any rate, it is to be found in you. The knowledge of your own ignorance, your own fragility of purpose, your own failure in aim and in achievement, is the first step in opening up the larger life which you hope at least is some day destined for you. And these injunctions of humility in à Kempis are as searching and as insistent as they are incomparably expressed: 'It does no harm if you rate yourself below everybody, but it does the utmost harm if you esteem yourself superior to even one.'

IV

The climax of the overcoming of self lies in the subdual of self with regard to God, the absolute subordination to him of all your needs and passions and desires. In other words, the final triumph of this essential struggle of life is the conquest of the will and the complete union of the frail human will with the all-dominating will of God. The basis of this last submission is an even more perfect development of the humility which we have already studied in connection with other human beings. If you are to esteem yourself nothing even in comparison with frail and feeble fellow-men, how abject is your nothingness compared to the prevailing grandeur of the source of all things. And to subdue and eliminate your own petty and misguided purposes for the larger working of his supreme designs is the great aim and effort of your existence: 'As to my own will what shall I say? It is the thing which my soul hates above all others.'

The obvious danger in this identifying and confounding your own will with God's is that you may reverse the process and assume merely that God's will is behind yours. Some of the most sincere and ardent of religious and mystical spirits, who were at the same time of vehement and self-assertive temperaments, have been peculiarly liable to this misinterpretation. In our own day, for instance, such a whole-souled religious worker as D. L. Moody was, as it seems to some of us, sometimes inclined to substitute Moody's intentions and purposes for those of God, or to mistake one for the other. And the same substitution runs often to astonishing lengths in the ecstatic proclamations of the mystics, as with Madame Guyon addressing the Deity: 'As for obedience, you made me practice it... with the submission of a little child, but also how much have you obeyed me yourself, or rather, O Lord, have you rendered my will marvelous by identifying it with your own!' It is well worth noting that this excess is not marked in à Kempis. His humility was so searching and so perfect that these subtle and roundabout self-assertions had no charm for him.

One of the most difficult and haunting elements of self to be overcome in these dealings with God is the instinct of intellectual research and investigation. There is the honest but exaggerated and uneasy effort to get at the truth. So many endless questions suggest themselves. There is such a vast reaching out of curious analysis to the end of the world, and beyond. How did we come to be, how did the universe come to be, how did God come to be, and where is it all tending to? There are questions of the Trinity, questions of the Atonement, questions of Christ's nature, questions of God's nature, and who shall answer them? To all which à Kempis's simple reply is, put these things aside and forget them. You have God's word, clear and intelligible, if you approach it in the right spirit: 'What shall it profit you to dispute loftily about the Trinity, if you lack humility, and so displease the Trinity?'

Or again, there is what professes to be vast theological investigation, carried on not from a sincere desire for truth, but simply to display one's own intellectual powers. 'There are those who do not walk with me sincerely, but who, led by a certain curiosity and arrogance, desire to know my secrets and to penetrate the heights and depths of God, all the time neglecting their own salvation.' They like to argue, they like to dispute, they like to convince and to triumph in convincing. Often they make a brilliant show and stir up a great tumult in the world, but the truth, the spiritual truth, is not in them.

The remedy for all the uneasiness and all the restlessness and all the vain intellectual aspiration is the simple, quiet repose of faith. '*Fruitive quiescere:'* it is impossible to translate it, but it appears that it is possible to feel it, with boundless spiritual peace. 'To abstain from vain spiritual wanderings and unprofitable arguments for the love of inward quietness.' Surely one whose soul has been torn for years by such wanderings and arguments may appreciate the eternal significance of that, and inward quietness may be the greatest of the gifts of God.

Only, when you think you have established such quietness, when you joyously hope that the supreme sacrifice has culminated, you so often find, in this imperfect and perishable world, that the peace has slipped away from you. The struggle is to be forever renewed, the battle is never finally won: 'Alas, alas, what bitterness of soul it brings, to labor and strive daily against one's self for the reward of eternal life.' The best of the saints, the most self-composed, the most serene, will sometimes cry with à Kempis: 'There is no love that is exempt from grief.'

Hence comes weariness, and depression, and discouragement, even a certain deadness and aridity, which seems at times to threaten the fatal *accidia*, the feeling that the eternal reward is unattainable and, worse still, if it is attained, it may not be worth the effort. The doubts and questions swarm, like pestilent insects, and all the devils in hell seem to be let loose to torment you.

The supreme and sure refuges are patience, and hope, and prayer. You know from long experience that these storms come, and that they pass: 'For after winter comes summer, after the night the day, and after a storm a great calm.' Accept these trials, as you accept others, as sent by God in his infinite wisdom for your good, wrap love and prayer about you like a comforting garment, and let the storm pass by.

So in a moment, perhaps when you least expect it, the sudden splendor of God overcomes you and fulfills you, and doubts and fears and anxieties are swept away: 'For, rapt out of themselves and swept beyond all merely personal pleasure, they plunge deep into the love of God and there are fruitfully at peace: there is nothing which can discourage or depress them, since they who are filled with eternal truth burn with the fire of inextinguishable love.'

It is true that those who are familiar with the abstract ecstasy of the more especially mystical saints may feel that à Kempis is somewhat too concrete. Though he everywhere and at all times regards Jesus as synonymous with God and as simply shepherding the soul to God, yet one may grow impatient with the persistent intrusion of Jesus as a personal figure, above all in that fourth book of the *Imitation*, with which one would sometimes hope that à Kempis had nothing to do. Also, there is a rather too frequent introduction of a very concrete heaven, that wearisome and uncomfortable vision of the future in which a huge aggregation of monastic and monotonous saints are eternally engaged in singing hymns which might in the end wear out the most devoted piety.

In other words, lovers of the high-wrought, perplexing ecstasy of Eastern Pantheism and of mystics like Saint Catherine, or Molinos, or Madame Guyon, those who take delight in the curious attempt to merge multiplicity in Unity and the distracting many in the eternal One, will sometimes find à Kempis a little unsatisfying. Certainly he does not indulge in the complicated raptures and speculations of Molinos: 'So that the soul must find itself dead to its will, desire, endeavour, understanding, and thought; willing as if it did not will; desiring as if it did not desire; understanding as if it did not understand; thinking as if it did not think; without inclination to anything; embracing equally contempt and honours, benefits and corrections. O what a happy soul is that which is thus dead and annihilated! It lives no longer in itself, because God lives in it.'

And it may well be, as many of his admirers contend, that à Kempis is more sane and reasonable than those who go to such intellectual and spiritual excesses. Yet, all the same, if you watch him carefully, you will find that he too has his moments when the personal and the concrete are burned away and desire and thought and life are dissolved in more intimate union: 'Then the soul begins to pant and long after and vehemently to be in love with this Good, wherein is all and every good, and with this Joy, wherein is all and every joy; with this One, wherein are all things both great and small, high and low; and yet this One is not any one thing of all the things that are created, but is supereminently beyond the form of any human conception whatsoever; it is the beginning and the end of all those goods and felicities that have been created thereby.'

What can be grander than to believe that the whole solid fabric of the universe is built up upon this enduring One? Only, if the One fades away, what is there left?

v

Yet even for the profane, to whom mystical rapture, however alluring, is a little unsubstantial, the *Imitation*, and in a less degree the other writings of à Kempis, retain a singular enchantment, because of their extraordinary qualities of literary beauty, which make the *Imitation* one of the masterpieces of the world. It is style that makes books live, and though style is inextricably bound up with thought and matter, thought and matter rarely have enduring significance without it. Assuredly in the *Imitation of Christ* every device and resource of literary art is employed to accomplish the one object which the author feels to be above every other.

There is the mere arrangement of the words, which makes so much of the charm and subtle impressiveness of the older Latin. Mediæval Latin is far freer and simpler and more modern than that of the Augustan Age, but à Kempis takes the language and moulds and fashions it to his purposes with a daring and a facility unusual to his contemporaries. Consider a sentence like this, which Cicero would never have written, yet which is so astonishingly effective: '*Vere ineffabilis dulcedo contemplationis tuae, quam largiris amantibus te.*' And again, there is the rhythm; always simple, brief, direct sentences, yet with a clinging sweetness of cadence that gives to prose almost the magic of poetry. And there are strange effects of rhyme, of assonance, also, so elaborate and complicated that they misled the German scholar Hirsche into the attempt to prove that the author of the *Imitation* was often writing actual verse. Hirsche shows all the exaggerations of German erudition, though his work is of extreme value as demonstrating the identity of authorship in à Kempis's various writings. But if à Kempis was not writing deliberate poetry, he at least understood all the subtlest secrets of literary effect. How skillful is his use of antithesis, of repetition, of the crowding, hammering accumulation of words, only oftentimes to conclude with a single light touch which goes as straight to its mark as a feathered arrow!

The remarkable thing is that, with all this skill and variety of artistic resource, the book cannot in any possible way be called artificial. On the contrary, it is the most perfect model of simplicity and naturalness, because the author, artist as he may be by instinct, is so possessed and overpowered

by his passion for conveying God to others and to
the whole wide world. Most characteristic of this
simplicity is the structure of the books and of the
chapters and the way they are built up. There is no
elaborate or systematic argumentation, no attempt
to work out an organized thesis to a definite and
preconceived end. A simple topic is selected for
each chapter, and the imagination and the feelings
play about it and about it with infinite wayward
subtlety and grace. And the same inspired, instinctive grace appears everywhere in the turn of
the phrases, which have so often a felicity that cannot be reduced to any artistic formula whatever:
'*In cruce infusio supernae suavitatis,*' '*fruitive
quiescere,*' '*qui adhaeret creaturae cadet cum labili,*'
'*cella continuata dulcescit et male custodita taedium
generat*' — you can hardly say what makes these
and so many others cling in the memory with
such compelling charm. And this combination of
art and simplicity suggests comparison with another
prose masterpiece, distinguished by these same elements, though differing from à Kempis in spirit as
widely as one book can differ from another. The
Daphnis and Chloë of Longus is a monument of Pa-
gan naturalism, but the delicate rippling cadences of
the Greek and the simple human touch all through
the book often remind one of the *Imitation.*

Where one finds such extraordinary literary
achievement, one cannot help asking one's self how
far it is conscious and intentional, how far the
writer thought of literary reputation, or at any rate

of literary ability and cleverness. It is hardly
necessary to say that à Kempis disclaims and condemns any such preoccupation with the utmost
energy. He realizes keenly the danger of it: 'If
anyone does well, if he reads well, or sings well, or
writes well; if he prays well, or studies well, or
preaches well, or celebrates well; behold, the Devil
at once hovers about him with vainglory.' But all
the more does he insist upon the necessity of getting
rid of that danger: 'Unhappy indeed is the man
who has made a name for himself in this world and
who makes fame his object.' These aims must be
rooted out and forgotten like every other earthly
desire. And in a way there is a certain splendor in
the thought that such a supreme flower of human
performance as the *Imitation* should remain in the
shadow of a dubious authorship, like the great
Gothic cathedrals, which it so much resembles in
spirit.

But it is impossible to feel that such a master
of words as à Kempis should not have been conscious of his mastery. You get the same impression
with other great religious writers. Paul was thinking of Christ first, but he was preaching Christ
with a marvelous gift of words, and he knew it,
whether he believed it came from the Holy Spirit
or not. So Augustine, so Fénelon, centuries later.
And the exquisite Francis of Sales played and toyed
with words with much the fascination that Shakespeare felt in them, as in his '*ne prenez pas le frifilis
des feuilles pour le cliquetis des armes.*' When à Kem-

pis speaks of the '*apices litterarum*,' 'the tips of letters,' he seems, whether he knew it or not, to suggest the delicate phrase with which Quintilian sums up all the magic of style, in speaking of beauty '*apicibus verborum ligata*,' clinging to the tips of words. And it must have been a perpetual revel to the solitary monk to spread God abroad with all the resources of splendor that the splendid Latin language could possibly be made to yield.

Yet back of all the beauty, whether conscious or not, there was always that profound, intriguing mystery of God, and the tender, solemn, entrancing fall of these magical phrases is like the choiring of the cherubim and seraphim in heaven. God is the secret, the supporting, the indispensable basis of it all. So we return to the note with which we began, 'Consider that God and you are alone in the universe, and you will have great peace in your heart.' Or, more largely and grandly: 'He will be but a petty spirit and cast down, who believes that there is anything great except the one immense, eternal Good. And whatever is not God is nothing, and should be accounted as nothing.' Or, in the equally solemn words of Amiel: 'There is but one thing needful — to possess God' — if you only can.

V
THE PRINCE OF DARKNESS
TALLEYRAND

CHRONOLOGY

CHARLES MAURICE DE TALLEYRAND PÉRIGORD.
  Born, Paris, February 2, 1754.
  At St.-Sulpice, 1770.
  Bishop of Autun, January, 1789.
  Member of Constitutional Assembly, 1789.
  In England, 1792, 1793.
  In America, 1794–1796.
  Foreign Minister, 1797–1799, 1799–1807.
  Married Catherine Worlée (Grand), September, 1802.
  Died, May 17, 1838.

TALLEYRAND

V

THE PRINCE OF DARKNESS
TALLEYRAND

I

SHAKESPEARE tells us that 'the prince of darkness is a gentleman.' Prince Talleyrand was a gentleman, at any rate in the narrower sense of the term. Also, he had a further amazing resemblance to the greater prince of darkness, not only in his apparent lack of moral convictions, but in the extraordinary murky obscurity under which he veiled his spiritual processes, even when he seemed to indulge in a careless and candid abandonment of speech, so that his close friend Madame de Staël could call him 'the most impenetrable and indecipherable of men.' Madame de Maintenon said of herself that she wished to remain an enigma to posterity. So Talleyrand is reported to have said: 'I wish that for centuries men may continue to discuss what I was, what I thought, and what I desired.' For the subtle inventions of human egotism are illimitable.

The almost centenary career of Charles Maurice de Talleyrand Périgord sweeps through as varied and complete a circuit as that of any human being who ever lived. Born in 1754, in the flower of the old French régime, his aristocratic connection en-

149

abled him in youth to enjoy the full relish of that brilliant period. Destined against his will for the Church and even rising as high as the bishopric of Autun, he threw it over and became politically active against his own order in the first years of the Revolution. He was in England on a diplomatic mission in 1792, and his further absence in that country and in America kept him out of the worst violence of the Reign of Terror. When he returned to France in 1795, he became Foreign Minister under the Directory, the Consulate, and the Empire. Talleyrand gradually drew away from Napoleon, and when he fell was a main instrument in the restoration of the Bourbons. Again for a brief period he was Foreign Minister under Louis XVIII. Then, after an interval of retirement, in 1830, when he was nearly eighty years old, he went as ambassador to England and performed the most distinguished service of his career. He died at his country estate of Valençay, in 1838, perhaps the most notable if certainly not the most admirable figure in Europe.

In considering Talleyrand's character it is necessary to take into account first of all the repression, the distortion, produced by the crippling lameness which hampered him all his life and the consequent indifference and estrangement of his family, who fixed their worldly expectations on his younger brother and turned the elder over to the ecclesiastical career he thoroughly detested. This family neglect has perhaps been exaggerated. It may have been no more than the usual treatment accorded to those in similar situations. But it was real, and on a temperament like that of Charles Maurice it must have had its effect.

Talleyrand himself liked to emphasize, and it may be to overemphasize, this element of family neglect and its influence in stunting and thwarting him. In his *Mémoires* he enlarges upon it, and he told Madame de Rémusat that after long years of separation from his parents, when he did come into contact with them, he was received 'as an unpleasant object and treated with the greatest coldness; that no word of affection or consolation was ever addressed to him.' He was shut off in a cloistered isolation and left to brood over his disappointed hopes and blighted ambitions.

How far his natural temper was really modified by these circumstances it is of course impossible to say. But there are many hints of an original kindliness, susceptibility, and even tender affection. In his *Mémoires* he refers to his mother in terms quite different from those suggested above: 'I preferred to go to my mother at the hours when she was alone. I could then better enjoy the graces of her mind. No one ever seemed to me to possess such fascinating conversation.' And at the other extremity of his career there is an even greater clinging regard for his niece by marriage, the Duchesse de Dino, and for his grand-niece Pauline. There seems to be a suggestion of natural profound sensibility which only needed development to have controlled the man's life. For example, he was a lover of animals, and left a definite legacy for the care of his dog Carlo.

But if the sensibility was there, it was crushed, distorted, subdued, till there was very little of it left. The youthful repression, the clerical isolation, produced an artificial stolidity, a habit of concealing, repelling, resenting emotions, which finally disposed of them almost entirely, and even showed in what seem pretentious comment, as in his account of his visit to the death-strewn field of Austerlitz with Marshal Marmont, when the Marshal could not withhold his tears, 'but as for me, I assure you it had no effect upon me whatever.' This artificial as it were make-up of character is admirably suggested by Madame de Rémusat: 'Monsieur de Talleyrand, more factitious than anybody else in the world, has contrived to make himself a natural character of a quantity of habits formed by design; he sticks to these in every situation, as if they had the force of an inborn temperament.'

Yet, for all this artificial stolidity the man in earlier years could write to a woman friend: 'Separated from all the interests of my heart, I am occupied only with the ideas that can restore me to them, and restore me to them permanently, so that I may live with them independently of the rest of the world and may form with a few friends a little globe of our own, quite impenetrable to all the follies and wickednesses that possess our unhappy Europe.' And in general it seemed as if the fine touch of a woman had the power to break through the hard enameled surface. There is the graceful story of the young abbé's first love-affair, the girl whom he meets in a church porch in a shower, convoying her home under his umbrella and confiding to her the secrets of his clerical loneliness. There is the long and varied series of more or less scandalous connections, scandalous even for a layman, touched occasionally with what seems like real passion, as in the ardent outcry: 'I love you with all my soul. I find all things endurable when I am near you. You! You! You! That is what I love more than anything else in the world.' And there is the supreme, dramatic culmination in the marriage, the marriage at fifty years old, of the cleverest man in the world, the man who seemed least likely to be duped, to a woman who, if not the stupidest in the world, was certainly stupid enough.

Curiously, something the same situation appears with that very first love-affair, for Talleyrand himself says of the young woman: 'I have since been told that she had not much sense: although I saw her almost daily for two years, I never noticed it.' And as to the showy, disreputable adventuress whom he finally married, when it was objected that she also had not much sense, he remarked, 'A clever wife often compromises her husband; a stupid one only compromises herself.' Madame Grand, *née* Worlée, was confessedly a woman of extraordinary physical beauty. Her hair especially was universally admitted to be dazzling, or, as the old dramatist has it, she had more hair than wit. But when the Emperor forced his minister to marry her or give her up, the passion had already more or less smouldered into a habit, and the minister must have realized that he was putting the fatal seal upon his rupture with the Church which refused to receive him back until the lady was finally consigned to oblivion. The explanation is to be sought in the strange, listless indifference which the man managed to unite with immense potentialities of power, as is delicately suggested in the comment of Madame de Rémusat: 'Monsieur de Talleyrand has a gentleness and great indifference in the daily habits of life. It is easy to dominate him by terrifying him, because he dislikes a disturbance.'

Even in his friendships with men, the earlier Talleyrand shows something of sensibility. Thus in his letters to Choiseul-Gouffier and to Narbonne there are touches of tender affection, as this to the former: 'I want you to receive from me a word that shall tell you that I love you with all my soul more than anything in the world and at all the moments of my life, be it fortunate, or anxious, or even unfortunate.' But as years passed on, these tender sentiments were mainly crushed out, or daubed over, or in some way disposed of, and the relation of friendship, as it appears in later years in the person of Montrond, is much less attractive. Montrond was a supremely clever rascal — almost as clever as Talleyrand himself, and perhaps even more rascally — and he was an immensely useful agent in shady transactions of all sorts. They used each other, and they respected each other's cleverness at any rate, but such words as esteem and affection hardly entered into the matter: 'M. de Montrond would never have told anyone else to trust M. de Talleyrand, nor M. de Talleyrand told anyone else to trust M. de Montrond.' The relation is well summed up in the little exchange of thrusts. 'Do you know why I like Montrond?' asked Talleyrand. 'Because he has not many prejudices.' And Montrond retorted, like a flash: 'Do you know why I like Monsieur de Talleyrand? Because he has no prejudices at all.'

The whole working and development of the stunting, thwarting spiritual process cannot be better indicated or analyzed than in Talleyrand's own account of it to Madame de Rémusat: 'You see, situated as I was, I had either to die of distress or to toughen myself so as not to feel the lack of what I could not have. I fell back on the toughening, and I am willing to agree with you that it was a mistake. It would perhaps have been better to suffer and to retain my faculty of feeling a little more deeply; for the indifference of the soul which you reproach me with has often disgusted me with myself. I have never loved others enough; but I have never loved myself enough either, and I have never taken enough interest in myself.'

II

Besides the blight resulting from youthful isolation, another most essential element has to be taken into account in considering Talleyrand's character, and that is his attitude toward money. Every period of revolution is always financially unstable. Fortunes are made and disappear with sudden, inexplicable rapidity and ease, and men quickly lose their sense of pecuniary scrupulousness unless they have unusual habits of restraint and conscience. Talleyrand never had any habits of this kind, and although the temper of his age has been hard pushed to make excuses for him, it is generally admitted that he would have been exceptional in any age. One of the most lenient of his biographers says that 'His great defect [was] a love of money, or rather a want of scruple as to how he obtained it.'

The root of the matter, of course, was that he wanted money, needed it, or thought he did, to gratify one of the most expensive sets of tastes with which a man was ever endowed. He liked splendid garments, he liked splendid houses, he liked to be elaborately served in every way. Especially, for himself and his guests he wanted the richest and most perfect table that could be supplied. All these things required money, and the first business of life was to get it. Riches, ever more riches, that was the cry. 'I have always been rich,' he said to Vitrolles. 'Even when I was an exile in America I had a habit of living, I had a house, just such as I have here.' On which Vitrolles remarks that 'the lie was bigger than the house.' And on another occasion Talleyrand is credited with saying that 'society is divided into two classes, the shearers and the shorn: one should always be with the first as against the second.' Whether he said it or not, it certainly represented the habitual policy of one whom Stendhal excellently summed up as 'a man of incomparable cleverness who never had enough money.'

The dire need appears most effectively in the appeal to Madame de Staël, when she was endeavoring to persuade Barras to give Talleyrand the post of Foreign Minister: 'My dear child, I have only twenty-five louis, not enough to go through the month. You know that, as I cannot walk, I have to have a carriage. If you do not find some means of giving me a suitable position, I will blow my brains out.' And the ecstasy resulting when the need was satisfied appears even more vividly in the almost delirious murmur, as the new minister drove in his carriage to accept the above appointment: 'We've got the place: now we must make *une fortune immense, une immense fortune, une immense fortune, une fortune immense.*' So that the same Madame de Staël, when she felt that she was treated with neglect and ingratitude, could cry out with some justice: 'Money, always more money, that is what you have sought all your life.'

There were three principal sources from which Talleyrand obtained his enormous supply of wealth.

In his early life and indeed always more or less he was, like Casanova, a gambler. Gambling of all sorts was a rage, a passion in the society of his youth, and he participated in it with the cool-headed ingenuity that characterized him in everything. I do not find any evidence that he was ever carried away. He was not the kind to stake his whole fortune on one throw — unless he had previous information as to what the turn of the throw might be. He himself says, 'Gaming occupies, but does not preoccupy.' He did not let it preoccupy him unduly. But it was always an amusement. Up to his very last days whist was his relaxation: 'Whist was the favorite distraction of the Minister. He remained faithful to it all his life. Also he played with passion at a game of dice, imported from England, called creps [*sic*]; he staked considerable sums on this.' And the amusement might be a moderate source of income, when other things failed.

But other things were vastly better than the gambling-table. There was speculation of all sorts, and wherever he happened to be, whatever he happened to be doing, Talleyrand had always a quick eye for a chance to make money. When he was an exile in America, the immense possibilities of the new country impressed him vastly, and he endeavored in all sorts of ways to get funds from his friends in France, which might be invested advantageously, for them — and for himself. And there was always the stock-market. A foreign minister has prodigious opportunities in this line. To be sure, some ministers have scruples. Talleyrand had none. And the story was that he kept the accommodating Montrond below in his carriage during diplomatic conferences, so that he might be sent off to buy or sell the instant a decision was arrived at.

Also, a foreign minister has other opportunities for financial gain, besides those directly affecting the stock-market, and Talleyrand was believed, perhaps we may say proved, to have taken advantage of these with a corruption and a venality almost unparalleled and incredible. An instance that comes home to readers of American history is the celebrated case of the X Y Z letters, in which Talleyrand tried to bargain with the American commissioners for immense sums to be paid to himself and to the Directors. But this is only one example of many. The man reached out and took from everybody, right and left, and when even he felt that he could not take with decency, there was always Montrond or somebody equally obliging to take for him. To be sure, there is the possible contention, pushed by Talleyrand himself to the limit, just as it was pushed by Ben Butler and others in America, that you are simply taking honest payment for honest services. But such a plea becomes ludicrous in face of the universal outcry of all honest contemporaries, summed up in the assertion that Talleyrand made his fortune by 'selling those who had bought him.' Chateaubriand said of him,

'When Monsieur de Talleyrand is not conspiring, he is bargaining.' Marshal Marmont said: 'Talleyrand combined in himself all that times past and present can offer as an example of corruption, having surpassed in this respect the limits known before his day.' And no one is more severe than Madame de Staël, who had loved Talleyrand and knew him thoroughly: 'He sold the Consulate, he sold the Empire and the Emperor, he sold the Restoration; he sold everything; and he will not cease to sell until his last day everything he can sell and even everything he cannot.'

The total of Talleyrand's accumulation from all these various sources, as reported, sounds often fabulous. All the different governments he served paid him huge pensions, and irregular sums kept rolling in from all quarters. It was said that his gains during the two years preceding the Consulate alone were thirteen million, six hundred and fifty thousand francs.

Sainte-Beuve, who discusses Talleyrand at unusual length, is unusually severe on this point of his financial corruption. The two men were alike in some ways, in their sexual irregularity and in their profound skepticism. But Talleyrand had little regard for truth, while Sainte-Beuve was almost meticulously veracious, and no man could ever charge Sainte-Beuve with violating his conscience for money. It is perhaps therefore natural that the critic should emphasize the deadly trail of infection which the greed for money is sure to carry

with it. Talleyrand is often credited with kindness
and even generosity, he says, and this cannot be
disputed. 'Yet, where their personal interest is
affected, Heaven preserve us from the kindness of
those who are fundamentally corrupt!' And the
gleam of gold shines everywhere in this description
which Madame de Staël gives of Talleyrand under
a feigned name: 'In the bottom of his heart he
loved nothing, believed in nothing, concerned himself about nothing; his one idea was to succeed, he
and his followers, in all the interests which make
up worldly life and fortune and popular repute.'
Yet after all perhaps he of us who has never done a
mean thing out of regard to money should be first
to cast a stone.

III

Among all Talleyrand's various needs for money
the chief was undoubtedly his constant require-
ment of social life and activity. He wanted to have
people about him always, to be bustling and stirring
among them. He could not feel that he was alive
himself unless he was an energetic agent in the
lives of others. He wanted to use them for his own
purposes, for his own advantage, he wanted to
manage them, to move them, to direct them, he
wanted to study them, with endless and inexhaustible curiosity. In an early page of his *Mémoires*
he says: 'I had still some years before me during
which I might share the life and pleasures of society,
without being obliged to arrange any of the deep

combinations required to satisfy the aspirations
of a serious ambition.' Such aspirations came on
soon enough, but the life and pleasures of society
had their appeal for him to the very end: 'It is
only through movement that one manages to
fortify one's self enough not to be engulfed by the
convulsions of the soul.' How much he knew of the
convulsions of the soul may be questioned, but he
certainly turned to movement as a lively and
constant refuge.

It is interesting to see how this social motive and
habit and atmosphere pervade and control every
aspect of the man's life. Take the intelligence.
Few could have been naturally quicker or keener.
When he was forced into a great library by the
dreaming solitude of his youth, he took to it readily.
'I spent my days there reading the productions of
great historians, the private lives of statesmen and
moralists, and a few poets. I was particularly fond
of books of travel.' Again, his ecclesiastical training led him through the wildernesses of theology
and he showed a ready aptitude for finding his way
there. When it becomes necessary to use his learning, he says, 'I employed all the arguments of
theology, which, when handled with a little judgment, are elastic enough to serve any purpose.'
Yet in all his long life I find no evidence of the
slightest intellectual enthusiasm. Books were useful. You could make good profit of them for handling men and women, you could make good talk of
them, which would help you to work your way in

the world. But books and libraries in themselves
— why bother with them? His vast indifference
shows in the brief comment, 'The ignorant do not
quite get at the truth; the wise often go beyond it.'
It shows still more, and more characteristically, in
another of his keen observations: which is quite
untranslatable: '*Voyez-vous, messieurs, il y a trois
savoirs: le savoir proprement dit; le savoir faire; et
puis le savoir vivre: les deux derniers dispensent bien
souvent du premier.*'

The same thing appears to be true of all æsthetic
interests. With nerves so quick and so variedly responsive, one would think that the man must have
been infinitely susceptible to beauty in all its forms.
If so, I find no trace of it. He liked a gorgeous
palace and a widely equipped and variegated park.
But he liked them wholly as a background to human diversions. It is impossible to imagine him
strolling in solitary woodland for the pure delight of
birds and flowers. He would have laughed at the
idea. He bought expensive pictures and statues
and liked to show them. I have no reason to suppose that he ever looked at them when he was alone
and the true lover of such things loves them chiefly
in solitude. I note but one passage in which he refers to music, but that one is immensely suggestive
and instructive, for the man, if not for the subject:
'Curiosity, much more than a decided taste for
music, took me also to all the learned and wearisome concerts that were given then.... I was careful not to have an opinion on French music, or on

Italian music, or on that of Glück. If, however, I had been obliged to pass an opinion, I should have felt inclined to say that, music being in general only a language which expresses, in an ideal manner, the sensations and even the sentiments that we experience, each country must have a style of music peculiar to itself.' It does not suggest any overwhelming intensity of rapture.

In short, Talleyrand's life was essentially, if not entirely, social, a life of contact, of human influence, of impression, of appearance, and the question immediately arises, How did he appear to his fellow human beings? In early years he seems to have been attractive in spite of his trailing infirmity. A certain aristocratic reserve did not injure him, and this easily softened and mellowed into a winning and even sympathetic response. The accounts of his appearance toward the end, when the efforts of his tribe of devoted valets sent him forth to dominate Paris and London society, are really remarkable, and in the vivid description of Raikes we read of 'his piercing gray eyes, peering through his shaggy eyebrows, his unearthly face, marked with deep stains, covered partly by his shock of extraordinary hair, partly by his enormous muslin cravat, which supports a large protruding lip drawn over his upper lip, with a cynical expression no painting could render; add to this apparatus of terror his dead silence, broken occasionally by the most sepulchral guttural syllables.'

Silence is here emphasized. But of course the

most permanently distinctive feature of Talleyrand was his talk, and it is the impression of this
that most lingers in the memory of men. Oddly
enough, silence was a conspicuous element of it.
He was said to be a most delightful talker with one
companion, 'delicious in the little square space of a
hackney coach.' In larger companies he rarely en-
grossed the conversation or asserted himself in
elaborate monologue: 'He will remain silent for a
whole evening, listening to what passes, and will
then perhaps make some very clever and pointed
remark, which every one will afterwards repeat.'
But rarely has the art of such pointed remarks been
more finished or more exquisite. The reported
achievement of many great talkers, Sydney Smith,
for example, is apt to lose its relish. But the keen
sayings of Talleyrand, worn as many of them are,
sparkle and glitter, even in the hundredth repetition, with a singular delicacy and cruel grace.

And through it all he had an inexplicable and
enthralling social charm. Even when you knew
perfectly well what he was, it was difficult to resist
him. Madame de Staël, who had every reason to
hate him, said, 'If you could purchase the conversation of Monsieur de Talleyrand, I should ruin
myself.' And another lady, who knew him almost
equally well, is even more enthusiastic: 'In spite of
everything he had a charm that I have never found
in any other man. You might be armed at every
point against his immorality, his conduct, his vices,
against everything he could be reproached with,

yet he won you just the same, as the bird is fascinated by the gaze of the serpent.' While there is the brief, effective phrase of the Pope, who again might not be expected to be wholly favorable: 'Monsieur de Talleyrand! ah! ah! may God have his soul; as for me, I am very fond of him!'

IV

With a person so thoroughly practical as Talleyrand, it might be expected that the gift of conversation, like all others, would be put to practical use, and what use could be more practical for it than politics? Thus from a very early period Talleyrand was tempted into the political world, and he never again stepped out of it. Probably few men have had such a vast and varied career of this order, from the tumult of the Revolution, through the shifting transformations that succeeded, up to the Empire, with its dramatic downfall, and the reigns that again followed. And through it all Talleyrand kept his eye on the multiform transformations that went on before him. 'He loves society and politics and when his time comes, you will see that he will die with a newspaper in his hand,' writes Madame de Lieven to Earl Grey.

As to his industry and power of labor in these political avocations accounts differ. He appeared indifferent and indolent. From his early model, the Duc de Choiseul, he learned the art of making others do all he could, and his celebrated injunction, '*Surtout, messieurs, pas de zèle*,' gave the impression of dilettante idleness. But undoubtedly he had that power of intellectual concentration which goes further in accomplishment than anything else. Also, though he had physical weaknesses, he had some advantages. For one thing, especially in later years, he could go almost without sleep, and would work till three or four o'clock in the morning and then get up again at six or seven. Also, he took much pride in a physical peculiarity, that of dropping every sixth beat of his pulse. He thought, or pretended to think, that this was one of Nature's conservative processes, and that the dropped beats were all stored up to increase his longevity and enable him to outwork other, more normal people.

As to abstract political ideas, there is not so much to be said in Talleyrand's case. In one department he appears as a strong and original thinker, that of finance. His dealing with financial problems under the Constituent Assembly was forcible, clear, and conservative, and he fought the tendency to fiat money with an energy and persistence that was perhaps hardly to be expected from such a source. His discussion of the financial and commercial conditions of America, when he was in that country, is most cogent and pointed, and shows a keen insight into the working of such matters as well as the power of expounding them. Also, on a somewhat larger economic basis, the paper which he read to the Academy after his return to France on the establishment and maintenance of colonies is shrewd and well thought out.

But as regards the broader fundamental problems of government, Talleyrand's thinking is barren and unproductive. To be sure, in his youth he seemed to enter with enthusiasm into the ideal movement of the Revolution and some of his biographers accept all his preaching of those days as gospel. To me it rings a little hollow. Very likely he thought he meant it and felt it, but I cannot believe that it took hold of him deeply.

And as the years went on, he grew more and more conservative, or rather, the intensely aristocratic bent of his inheritance and temperament more and more asserted itself. The world was made for his class and it was for the good of the world that his class should rule it. He could hardly conceive, and certainly could not support, any other solution. As he put it to Madame de Lieven: 'The old governments alone offer repose and happiness to individuals. Constitutions are follies; nations will have nothing to do with them, because they have the conservative instinct.'

So the sum of Talleyrand's political action may be said to have been balance, adjustment, arrangement, compromise, or, if the balance was violently distorted and thrown out, the effort to restore it and put things back where they had been. The aim of perpetual adjustment and his idea of the means of it are well indicated in a thoughtful sentence from one of his more formal addresses: 'The art of putting men in their right places is perhaps the first in the science of government. But the art of finding the place of malcontents is certainly the most difficult, and to present to their imaginations distant possibilities, perspectives to which their thoughts and their desires may attach themselves is, I think, one of the solutions of this social problem.'

The most fruitful, valuable, and constructive element of Talleyrand's political labor in these harmonizing directions was unquestionably his love for peace and his active working for it. He detested war, felt it to be stupid, disastrous, and utterly unnecessary, and such a disposition, in the riotous and bellicose world he lived in, was of the utmost utility. Thus his labors at the Congress of Vienna and again under the Restoration in 1830 were indisputably of profit, not only to France, but to Europe. To be a power for peace in the first quarter of the nineteenth century was almost as noble a distinction as it was in the first quarter of the twentieth.

And in working for peace Talleyrand displayed all the most notable gifts and aptitudes of the diplomat, so that he will probably always stand out as the most conspicuous example of the type. He had the inexhaustible patience, the indomitable persistence, the tireless readiness to accept defeat in the habit of perpetually renewed effort. He had the impenetrable reserve, the power of significant silence, and also the instinct of just the right word in the right place. But what is most astonishing of all is his repeated emphasis upon good faith and straightforward dealing. Again and again he asserts that the true secret of diplomacy is not petty ruse and ingenious trickery, but to come right out as man to man, to lay your cards squarely on the table, let the other fellow see what you have and ask for similar frankness from him. Surely there could not be a finer statement of this than the following passage on the qualities of a great foreign minister: 'He needs the faculty of appearing open yet remaining impenetrable, of being reserved with all the manifestation of candor... in a word, he must not cease for a moment in the twenty-four hours to be minister of foreign affairs. And yet all these qualities, rare as some of them may be, might not be sufficient, if good faith did not give them the guarantee of which they are almost always in need.' Sainte-Beuve smiles cynically at the good faith of a Talleyrand. Yet after all it seems that he was large enough to appreciate that when big people are working with big interests, open, straight-out, direct dealing has its advantages, even from the point of view of selfishness.

The most curious application of Talleyrand's passion for peace is in his relations with Napoleon. For it happened to this lover of peace to be consistently attached to the greatest fighter of the world. The consequence was that during the whole fifteen years of their connection the minister was, if not thwarting the policy of his chief, at any rate acting as a check upon it. To Napoleon it appeared, and especially afterwards, as if this meant a course

of persistent betrayal. And it is certainly a singular feature of Talleyrand's career that from first
to last he at least appeared to have betrayed a long
succession of leaders and always, invariably, to
his own advantage in the end. As Bulwer diplo-
matically expresses it: 'It was M. de Talleyrand's
fortune not merely at all times to quit a falling
party at the commencement of its decline, but to
stand firm by a rising party at the moment of its
struggle for success!'

Yet how endlessly curious it is to get the different
psychological points of view in these matters!
Napoleon and the rest, as they were betrayed,
loudly called it betrayal. Talleyrand quietly insisted that it was nothing of the kind. The highest loyalty in the world was the loyalty to one's
country, and from the beginning to the end he had
been faithful to France, had worked for France, had
only deserted those who had first deserted her. As
he put it squarely: 'I have never kept fealty to any
one longer than he has himself been obedient to
common sense. But, if you judge all my actions by
this rule, you will find that I have been eminently
consistent.' And he justifies himself further by an
ingenious application of a saying of Machiavelli,
surely good authority for political duplicity:
'Every mutation furnishes material for making
another.' It is interesting to find even so robust
and downright a spirit as the Duke of Wellington
defending Talleyrand's public conduct, and the
defense brought tears to Talleyrand's eyes with the

affirmation that there was no other statesman in Europe who would speak well of him.

Yet with it all one feels that the betrayals were there and no amount of ingenious apology can explain them away. Self was at the bottom of it, self-advancement, self-aggrandizement, even when it was not self in its lowest form of money greed. The curious thing is that this is quite compatible with what is suggested in Talleyrand's remark to Madame de Rémusat, already quoted, that he had never cared enough about himself. He did not care so very much about himself, but he cared infinitely less about others. And it is precisely in this very not caring, this profound spiritual indifference, that I should seek the explanation of the further curious fact that Talleyrand, with all his varied political activity, never manifested the slightest gift of leadership. He was always working for his own hand and by himself. No one believed in him or followed him or trusted him. There was never any serious question of putting him at the head of things, except for the brief accident of the Provisory Government in 1814. No one would have wanted to see him in such a position. I am not aware that he had a single devoted follower except Montrond, who was patently interested only in what he could get. Talleyrand had many of the qualities of great success, but the qualities of the leader of men were distinctly not among them.

TALLEYRAND

V

It is in this aspect of leadership that Talleyrand is most strikingly contrasted with Napoleon, who was one of the greatest of born leaders of men. And in general it is not the least interesting element in Talleyrand that he was so long and so intimately associated with the great Emperor whose soul is assuredly one of the most curious subjects of study that the world affords. The two men were both keen and profound observers, they had the best possible opportunities for observing each other, and they uttered their observations freely for the benefit of careful recorders who have passed them on to us.

They both admired each other, each appreciating in the other the qualities that he himself lacked, and at the same time they both despised each other thoroughly. There were times when Napoleon was discontented, could not himself see what it was in Talleyrand that went so far. He complained that 'he could not conceive how people found M. de Talleyrand eloquent. He always turned round the same idea.' Then again he was forced to praise the infinite ingenuity and adaptability that had so often served his purposes: 'He is a man of intrigues, of a great immorality, but of extraordinary intelligence, and certainly the most capable of all the ministers I have had.' Yet all the time underneath there was a profound mistrust, which in the after reflections of later years broke out into a poignant regret: 'If I had hanged two men, Talleyrand and Fouché, I should still be on the throne.' And the deeper, more general attitude well appears in the observation of Madame de Rémusat, which applied more to Talleyrand than to anyone else: 'What Bonaparte dreaded most in the world was that anybody near him should use, or even possess, the faculty of judging him.'

Assuredly no one exercised that faculty with more cool and relentless insight than Talleyrand, and the petulant sensibility of his master was no doubt perfectly well aware of those keen eyes always watchful to penetrate into the inmost recesses of his hidden motives. In the early days Talleyrand, like so many others, came more or less under the spell of that exciting, infectious, magnetic spirit, which had always the gift of imparting to even the dullest the inspiration of its own magnificent dreams. And Talleyrand writes, in 1797, 'For all the rest surrender yourself to your own combinations: they will be sure to have the character of grandeur and stability that you know how to give to everything.' And in many respects the admiration continued till the end, so that the cynical Montrond could even check the expression of it by the cool comment: 'You may well eulogize him, for you have done him damage enough.' But as time went on, the critical observer grew increasingly aware of the defects and especially of the fatal and inevitable consequences of them. It seems a little strange to have Talleyrand reprehending anyone for trickery and treachery, yet the device by which the Spanish princes were ensnared at Bayonne seemed to him not only villainous but impolitic: 'Victories don't suffice to efface such things as these, because there is something which it is impossible to describe that is vile, deceitful, cheating!' And indeed Talleyrand later took the same position with regard to the execution of the Duc d'Enghien, though it seems likely that he had a considerable hand in that matter at the time. As to the general, final judgment of Napoleon's career, perhaps it could not be better summed up than in his minister's brief and overwhelming verdict: 'What an anticlimax in history! To give one's name to a series of adventures instead of fastening it upon one's age. When I think of all that, I am overcome with profound regret.'

With this perpetual play of cool mutual judgment in the background, nothing can be more impressive than the direct working of these two intensely contrasted and intensely significant temperaments upon each other, for the force of circumstances was such that the two were violently thrown together at every step. Napoleon constantly turned to Talleyrand for advice and assistance, knowing that there was no one who could help him out of a critical diplomatic situation with such facility and effect. Even after Talleyrand had ceased to be foreign minister and was exercising court functions only, the Emperor

appealed to him and would have liked to have
him back, if Talleyrand would have agreed.
Yet all the time Napoleon was utterly mistrustful,
knew that all sorts of intrigues and certainly
thieveries were going on behind his back, and when
his temper gave way he would burst out into the
most violent and abusive tirades, such as his native
Corsican insolence taught him to use when he
needed them: 'You are a robber, a coward, a man
without faith; you do not believe in God.'

And all the time Talleyrand maintained his utter
impassivity and said nothing, or merely murmured,
'What a pity so great a man should have been so
ill brought up!' When the storm had passed, he
would regain his supremacy with some touch of
the wheedling grace of intimate comprehension
that always linked the two together. And under
cover of these things he managed probably to give
his master more needed and useful advice than he
ever received from any other quarter. The skill
and tact with which it was done appear in Talleyrand's own remark: 'I am of the opinion that
one can say anything to the Emperor, because his
superiority is so great that he will understand
everything.' Yet, however impassive you may be
in appearance, perhaps all the more because you
are impassive, such treatment tells in the end,
and, human nature being what it is, it is not altogether surprising that Napoleon's downfall should
have come to Talleyrand like a personal deliverance
and a personal revenge.

TALLEYRAND

The keenness and subtlety of Talleyrand's observation of Napoleon impels one to consider more generally his observation of mankind at large. Assuredly no human being ever had more opportunity for such observation. His long sojourn in various countries, his contact with all sorts of people, high and low, afforded him an almost unequaled basis of judgment, and it cannot be questioned that he had the gift to take advantage of it. From the fierce excesses of the French Revolution to the polished artificiality of English court society, all circles had been opened to him and all circumstances had become familiar.

Also, he not only had the opportunities, but he profited by them, even reveled in them. Observation of life and character was an infinite entertainment to him, perhaps the only entertainment that did not fail, as the years went on. To discriminate, to distinguish, to analyze, was an unfailing joy: 'What attention is not required to discover the springs of these passions so varied in their action, to distinguish, to separate the effects that belong to different causes, and in their apparent contradictions to apprehend what is passing and occasional so as not to confound it with what is permanent and independent of the mobility of circumstances!' And the profit of such analysis is as great as the amusement. When you want to make use of men for your purposes, above all when you want to make money by them, you must watch their every action and their every motive with the most particular care.

With Talleyrand's temperament and with his vast experience, it is sometimes surprising to hear him speak as he so often does of individuals with admiration and esteem. It is like his enthusiasm for the working of *bonne foi* in diplomacy. It is not only of the friends of his youth that he speaks with cordial admiration, of Narbonne, of Choiseul, but there is the same extravagant praise of Fox, of Hamilton, of various others. There seems at times to be a touch of almost naïve candor about him, as when he says of himself: 'Pray tell me what is true of all this, for I always believe what you say. When I like a person, I believe him; sometimes I have been mistaken; nevertheless such is my nature.'

But the general tone is not quite so optimistic. After all, with an intelligence like Talleyrand's, the dislike of being duped is the prominent impulse, and he did not propose to be duped into any undue confidence in the ability or the honesty of mankind. You should treat all men as if they were intelligent, and commend them as if they were wise, but in your inmost thought your conclusions were likely to be very different, and if government was your business, you must not assume or expect too much: 'If you mean to legislate practically for men, you must treat men as they always have been and always are.' The remark is just, and far-reaching, but perhaps not too encouraging.

TALLEYRAND

The curious exception to Talleyrand's general contempt for humanity is his tenderness, not to say blindness, with regard to women. We have already seen his comment about his early love, that some people thought her stupid, but for his part he never noticed it, and the same indifference extended to the divine stupidity of the lady he married. Whether he was eighteen, or eighty, if you had charm, you could win him, and he was as much infatuated by the Duchesse de Dino and Pauline, as by the young woman under the umbrella fifty years earlier.

Finally, one asks how this supreme analyst stood in the crucial analysis of all, that of one's self. Here again, as with the women, he does not seem quite so supreme. Whether it was that there was less profit in self-analysis, or whether he thought the particular subject he was concerned with would not bear too much inspection, or whether he really dissected more than he revealed, it is difficult to say. But the five vast volumes of his *Mémoires* are about as barren of self-revelation as so many pages could well be. And the more casual glimpses of him that occur so widely are hardly more fruitful. Talleyrand, for instance, would have been utterly incapable of the bare and terrible self-exploration with which Napoleon tears the mask from his soul in the passage in which he proclaims to Talleyrand himself: 'Frankly, *I am a contemptible coward, essentially contemptible:* I give you my word that I should have no repugnance to committing what the world calls a dishonorable action.' Self-analysis such as this was beyond Talleyrand's reach or desire. In one of his bitter and caustic touches, he is said to have remarked, when someone insisted that Fouché had a great contempt for human nature, 'To be sure: he has made a careful study of himself.' But I think if Talleyrand had made a more careful and more profound study of himself, he would perhaps have had less contempt for human nature and would at any rate have made a more profitable use of it.

VII

After such consideration of Talleyrand's acute judgment of his fellow-men, one turns naturally with much curiosity to his judgment of God, but it is evident that this subject interested him at all times far less than the other. There was more than a profound, fundamental skepticism, more than the rooted indifference, as he expressed it, 'the discouragement of a man who has been a witness of everything and has seen through everything,' there was the bitter rebellion against the oppression and repression of his youth, which kept him in early years consistently hostile to the Church and everything connected with it. As he himself says of that formative period: 'More thoughtful than is usual at the age I was then, rebellious, but powerless, indignant, without either daring to or being justified in displaying my indignation.'

The estrangement from all religious matters

seemed for long years to be complete. And the man's nominal position as Bishop of Autun and his use of that position in connection with the Revolutionary attempt to detach the State from the Church, culminating in his consecration of the State bishops and his performance of Mass at the great ceremonial in honor of the destruction of the Bastille, in 1790, only made the inconsistency more glaring and hideous. Of all this even the supremely skeptical Sainte-Beuve says: 'One suffers at such a parody. Even if all religion is put aside, common decency revolts.' And the estrangement seemed to be finally perfected by Talleyrand's marriage, though this took place without much enthusiasm on his part and when his attitude was already beginning to be somewhat uncertain.

For the most curious thing in the whole matter is his gradual return to the Church in his last days. This does not seem to have been any question of spiritual disturbance, any revival of emotional associations of an earlier time. If these things had any pull for him, it does not appear. But what did hold him, and held him more and more, was the consciousness of belonging to the aristocratic class which had kept the old world, his world, together, and religion was above all things the stamp of that class. 'There is nothing less aristocratic than incredulity,' he said; and even more profoundly characteristic is the remark, 'I have but one fear, that of doing something to violate the proprieties.' Now the Church was the

essence and the acme of all proprieties. Therefore
let us be reconciled to the Church even to the extent of forgetting that inconvenient, long-neglected
wife. And yet — and yet — let us put it off till
the last moment. And he did, not signing the re-
cantation of his errors till his weeping women
feared it would be too late.

But under it all I cannot divine very much of
God. It was all done in the spirit of Voltaire:
'You are right, we ought to come back into the
sphere of the Church, we ought to die in the religion of our fathers and of our country: if I had been
born on the banks of the Ganges, I should want to
expire holding the tail of the sacred cow in my
hand.' The sacred cow, or the sacred wafer, what
difference did it make to Charles Maurice de Talleyrand Périgord? And in a passage of unusual pene-
tration and self-analysis, he strikes the final,
desolating balance as to God and as to himself:
'Here are eighty-three years passed. I do not
know whether I am satisfied when I recapitulate
how so many years have slipped away, or how I
have managed to fill them. How many useless
agitations! How many efforts that have been un-
fruitful, tiresome complications, exaggerated emotions, powers wasted, gifts cast away, hostilities
inspired, solid poise overturned, illusions destroyed, passions and desires satiated and rendered vain! And what is the result of it all?
Moral and physical fatigue, complete discouragement for the future, and profound disgust for the

past.' Such seems to be the epitaph and the epitome of the Prince de Talleyrand, after eighty-three years of piling up a fortune and duping God and man.

VI
GOD AND THE WORLD
FÉNELON

CHRONOLOGY

François de Salignac de La Mothe Fénelon.
   Born, Château de Fénelon, August 6, 1651.
   Ordained priest, 1674(?).
   Superior of Nouvelles Catholiques, 1678.
   Preceptor of Duc de Bourgogne, 1689.
   Met Madame Guyon, 1688.
   Wrote *Télémaque*, 1693, 1694.
   Quietest controversy, 1697–1699.
   Exiled to diocese, August, 1697.
   Death of Duc de Bourgogne, 1712.
   Died, January 17, 1715.

FRANÇOIS DE LA MOTHE FÉNELON

VI

GOD AND THE WORLD
FÉNELON

I

IF EVER there was a born saint, it was Fénelon. But his saintliness did not take the path of eschewing the world, but the far more difficult one of overcoming it, though there were times when the world seemed likely to have the better. The saint was a high-born gentleman. He had temptations to success in literature. He had temptations to success in society. He had supreme temptations to success in statesmanship, to the making over of the world on the model of God, and when his hopes in this regard were suddenly and utterly blasted, he had temptations to despair. But the love and hope of God finally conquered and he went out of life more of a saint than he came into it.

François de Salignac de La Mothe Fénelon was born in 1651. He belonged to an old and distinguished family, but money was not very abundant, and the natural recourse for younger sons in such a case, when they did not care for the Army, was the Church. Fénelon's acceptance of the ecclesiastical career, however, was not a mere choice of evils, and from beginning to end he loved and followed it with a natural, instinctive ardor. Only he loved other things also, loved the glitter and sparkle of well-ordered words, loved the society of men and women and to be loved by them, loved to play a great part, not only in the Church but in the world. His advancement was steady and sure. He was personally acceptable everywhere, in the court as well as in the cloister. While still an abbé, he obtained positions of considerable importance, and finally, in 1689, King Louis the Fourteenth appointed him tutor to his grandson, the Duke of Burgundy, who, much more than his father, was looked upon as the future hope of the kingdom. In 1695, Fénelon became Archbishop of Cambrai, near the borders of Holland, and in every respect a brilliant future seemed assured for him. But meantime, through his wholly spiritual association with Madame Guyon, he had become involved in the Quietist controversy, and, after a long and bitter dispute with the great Bossuet, Bishop of Meaux, Fénelon got the worst of it. He was still, however, preceptor to the Duke, and when the Duke's father died, it looked as if Fénelon might become the leading man in the kingdom, a sort of second Richelieu. Then the Duke also died, and Fénelon's future went out like a blown candle. Though he continued externally active and beneficent in his diocese, there was little left for him in this world, and he died in 1715, a few months before King Louis.

Perhaps the most significant and characteristic element in Fénelon is his power over human souls, both as to their conduct for this world and their spiritual advantage for another, and in this latter sphere he practiced the difficult and exquisite art which the Catholic Church knows as 'direction' almost as skillfully, if not quite so exclusively, as Saint Francis of Sales. When one is in entire agreement with the remark of Madame Guyon, 'What I relish is the souls of human beings,' one is enchanted, fascinated by the opportunity for soul-study which such direction gives. The instinct of self-confession is deeply implanted in all of us, especially when we are in distress or difficulty, and provided only that we can trust him to whom we are to confess. When the Church authorizes an impersonal ear and an impersonal heart to listen to us and comfort us, there is no limit to what we are ready to reveal. Think of the mine of curious discovery that is thus laid open to a born naturalist of souls. And when to the mere curiosity of scientific investigation is added the passion for helping, for healing, for guiding souls into the heavenly road which has been clearly and divinely mapped out for you, it seems as if there could be no richer or more satisfying occupation in the world.

Also, it is useless to deny that such an art of spiritual guidance carries with it the gratification of the desire for power, which is one of the strongest passions of the human heart. The best, the most self-forgetful, the humblest of religious advisers must feel a certain exaltation in the sense that scores of suffering human beings lift up their eyes and their hearts to God through him. As Lemaître puts it, in his delightful study of Fénelon: 'In a priest personal ambition may be intimately intermingled with his sacerdotal function, and the delight of dominating men (and women) with the relish of directing and saving souls.' Fénelon's friend Madame Guyon, herself a widely practicing directress of all sorts of people, frankly expresses this sense of power: 'Our Lord, together with the weakness of a child, gave me also the power of a God over souls, so that with a single word I can put them in pain or in peace, according as may be necessary for their good.' And what black art of magic could offer more resources of spiritual intoxication? Take another, much later, Protestant practitioner of direction, D. L. Moody: 'It is a greater thing to have power over a living, sinning, God-hating man than to quicken the dead.' And though Fénelon does not enlarge upon this aspect of his supreme life work, it is everywhere evident that he appreciated it fully.

Yet with Fénelon, as with any director worthy of the name, the power, however splendid and seductive it might be, was to be consecrated by devotion to the service of God. When looked at in this way, the sense of responsibility was even greater than the sense of power. As Fénelon himself puts it, 'The business of direction is not an affair into which any human consideration should enter, however innocent and well-regulated; it is a dealing based

on pure faith, on heavenly grace, on unalloyed
fidelity and utter death to all feeling of self'; and
again, even more forcibly, 'You must simply become an incarnation of spiritual law, which shall
carry religion into every heart; you must die un-
ceasingly to yourself, in order to lead others to
enter into that practice of subdual which is the
foundation of Christian life.' And it is evident
enough that the number of spiritual directors, even
when trained and inspired for the purpose, who
could live up to such an ideal must always be in-
sufficient. Fénelon deplores their scarcity with
almost despondent frankness: 'O my God! if I
ever ventured to complain of you, the only thing I
should find fault with would be that you do not
give your Church enough of these men.... Where,
O my God! are the burning and shining lamps,
placed in your house to warm and to enlighten
your children? How scanty the number of them!
Where may they be found?'

It is hardly necessary to say that, in making this
complaint, Fénelon was not thinking of himself,
or in any way holding himself up as a model.
Nevertheless, few men could have been more adapted
for such work than he was, by position, by training, and above all by natural temperament. As
one of his friends said of him, 'He excelled in the
knowledge of men, he could almost read what was
going on in your heart.' And the knowledge was
used, without affectation, without undue solemnity, but by every possible method of ingenious

pressure, to turn the hearts into the way which Fénelon passionately desired to have them follow.

There was quiet, subtle, tender, almost imperceptible persuasion, applied at just the effective moment which D. L. Moody was later so skillful in selecting. Some souls did not need, would not bear, to be urged, to be commanded, to be terrified, but had to be dealt with gently: 'One should not act as judge, nor insist upon being believed. One should say what one thinks, not as it were with authority and taking it for granted that he who listens will at once be made over, but simply, as if to relieve one's own heart… and not to be remiss with a person one loves…. When one gives counsel in this spirit, one gives it gently, and it finds its way into the soul through love.'

And again, with the sluggish, with the indolent, with those who were absorbed in the things of this world and their own enjoyment of it, he could stir and startle and arouse with words that flamed like fire in their urgent appeal. What he fought and battled with and strove to subdue at all times, in others and in himself, was the *moi*, the hideous, subtle, encroaching, involving I. How different from the attitude of today, which steadily seeks the acceptance and development of self, in all its fullest and richest powers. Fénelon tracked out and hunted down the self of this world, even in its most hidden fastnesses of apparent unselfishness: 'You love yourself even to the extreme point of taking credit for not loving yourself at all.…

It is, after all, the self that makes you think you are so sensitive and so responsive and so thoughtful for others.'

And in the fierce, unremitting contest with the lurking, monstrous self, this gentle, tender spirit could be severe, austere, violent, could reprehend roughly, almost cruelly, when he felt that he was dealing with the hardened and corrupt, who could be reached and touched in no other way. Thus to one recalcitrant he could cry: 'What does the Lord owe you? Nothing but hell, and a hell even more rigorous than should be the lot of most.' And again, 'It is only God who can effect these great changes in a soul so far astray and so bitterly hardened as yours.'

The way to make even these severe rebukes acceptable and tolerable and beneficial is to make them in the right spirit; that is, to make it all the time clear that you are speaking, not from any lofty plane of superiority, but with sympathy, with understanding, with a keen and ample sense of human frailty in yourself, since you are always capable of falling into the errors and weaknesses that you are chiding in others. In short, the supreme art in this matter of direction is to make men feel that you enter into their souls through the similarity of your own. As Moody expressed it years later: 'You must put yourself in their places. I tell you, if we only put ourselves in their places, we can succeed in bringing souls to Christ.' And in this exquisite art of putting himself in others' places Fénelon never had a superior. Everywhere in the *Spiritual Letters*, in which he exercises the art of directing souls, he unveils the inner working of his own heart with the most candid and enchanting clarity. He is in all points tempted as we are, and he makes us feel that he is so. The weaknesses, the pettinesses, the worldliness, the selfishness, that he reprehends in others are all the time lurking in himself; he is perfectly aware of it and admits it: 'It is true, Madame, that self-love often leads me astray: I act often from human prudence and for a merely human purpose.' And the human weakness is marvelously analyzed in passages like the following: 'For me, when I suffer, I can think of nothing but unlimited suffering; and when the time of consolation returns, my nature fears to grasp it, lest it should prove to be an illusion which may surprise me with more agonizing torment when the suffering is renewed.'

It is hardly necessary to say that Fénelon was just as direct, sincere, and positive in dealing with the great as in dealing with the little. His own social standing made this comparatively easy for him, and he could speak to lords and ladies as their equal because their speech and their manners and their habits were naturally his. He did not hesitate a moment to urge or even order dukes and princes into the narrow way, and sometimes even it seems as if he took a peculiar pleasure in doing so. When a great lady said to Moody, 'Mr. Moody, no one ever talked to me like this before,'

he answered quietly, 'Then it was quite time somebody did so.' Fénelon appears often to have had
much the same feeling as Moody. When he wants
to arouse a *grand seigneur* to a sense of his spiritual
duties, he cries: 'After the many benefits you have
received, you have more need than another to be
cast down from on high, because you need to have
your loftiness, which is extreme, brought low, and
to have your pride crushed, though it constantly
tends to spring up again.' Even to his dear friend
and supporter the Duke of Chevreuse he does
not fear to speak out with withering frankness:
'Reason little, and do much, whereas, on the contrary, you are always tempted to reason a great
deal, and while you are reasoning so much, you
accomplish very little.' And the most astonishing
example of his severe treatment of the great is the
letters he wrote to Madame de Maintenon, when
she was practically Queen, and to the King himself,
letters in which he lays down the law to them with
the passionate vehemence of a Hebrew prophet.

As with Francis of Sales, it is especially interesting to watch Fénelon's dealings with women, and
in one case as in the other, though the intimacy
of the dealings sometimes suggested scandal, there
is not the faintest shadow of a pretext for it.
There were moments when the feminine peculiarities irritated Fénelon, as they did Francis, though
not quite to the point of Saint Jerome, who ex-
claims, 'What shall we do with these wretched
little women, saturated with petty sins, who veer

with every breeze of doctrine, who are always asking questions, and never learn anything from the
answers?' In the same spirit Fénelon murmurs
about 'women who think everything that is serious and not amusing too cold and dry, and who
believe that you are not listening to them if you do
not let them tell you a hundred things that are
perfectly futile before you get to that which really
counts.' Yet in Fénelon, as in Francis, there
was something essentially feminine, which enabled
him to enter into feminine troubles and difficulties
and to clear them up or smooth them away with a
delicacy of touch that made the hearer devoted to
him forever.

In short, it is easy to understand the charm of
the business of direction, of soul management, for
one so perfectly adapted to it, a charm which in
his youth made him eager to go as a missionary to
Canada or to the East, and to his last day kept him
exercising an irresistible spiritual influence over
everyone about him. There was the profound and
varied interest of studying hearts, there was the
endless excitement of controlling and dominating
them, there was the pleasure of contributing to
their eternal felicity, and above all there was the
sense of serving God in the way in which he most
wished to be served.

II

It is evident that in this art of spiritual direction
everything depends upon the director, and hence

one naturally turns from what Fénelon did to what
he was. It may be said that he was one of the most
multiple, complicated souls that ever lived, and the
complication cannot be better suggested than in
the portrait left us by Saint-Simon, the greatest of
all painters of soul and body both: 'This prelate
was a tall man, lean, well made, pale, with a large
nose, and with eyes from which fire and intelligence poured like a torrent, a face such that I have
never seen another like it and that you could not
forget when you had seen it once. It suggested
everything and in it contraries did not conflict
with each other. There was gravity and gallantry,
there was seriousness and gayety, there was at
once the scholar, the bishop, and the grand gentleman. What predominated in it, as in his whole
person, was subtlety, wit, grace, good taste, and
above all a certain nobleness. It required an effort
to turn your gaze away.' To which should perhaps
be added, more simply, that, whatever you might
be, you felt a response in him: as soon as you looked
at him, you felt at home.

Fénelon's intelligence is perhaps as characteristic as any aspect of the man. He was well and
solidly educated, in literature, especially the classics, and in philosophy and history and theology.
He could quote the classic authors, and loved to do
so. One of his earliest attempts at writing was an
elaborate discussion of the philosophical views of
Malebranche, and his own philosophical attitude
was largely founded on the then recent theorizing

of Descartes. But more and more he came to distrust the intelligence and to warn his followers against the dangerous, disastrous snares involved in a too slavish subservience to the reasoning faculty: 'One makes one's self an idol of one's intelligence as a woman who thinks she is beautiful makes herself an idol of her face.' Yet all the time you feel that his dread of this intellectual subtlety and power lies largely in his sense of its fascination and influence for himself. No man ever had a keener, more penetrating, more supple intelligence than he, and, above all, it was immensely active, always working, working, working, to some remote and some profitable end. He might despise it and contemn it, as no doubt he sincerely did. All the same, he was a creature of brains as well as of spirit, and it is delightful to follow the endless interplay of the two upon each other.

But Fénelon was not only a creature of brains, he was eminently a man of the world and conversant with the thick of it. It must never be forgotten that he was a born aristocrat, for he himself never forgot it. He was humble, he was democratic, he recognized in himself all that constitutes common humanity: 'If I examine my conduct and my prayers, I shall find nothing that is not in the common heart of everyday Christians.' Yet he was a gentleman, and he knew it, and the honor of a gentleman prevailed with him, as well as the duty of a Christian. He would not have admitted that

the two could conflict, would have fully accepted
Dekker's lovely description of Christ as

> The first true gentleman that ever breathed;

but when there was a divergence, the gentleman's
honor had its way, and he stuck to Madame Guyon
against the dictates, not only of professional obliga-
tion, but of common sense. And, as a gentleman, he
had access to the best society of France, moved in
it with ease and assurance, and under all circumstances made himself at home.

He had the exquisite art of conversation in the
highest degree. He loved it, and à Kempis's sense
of the sacredness of silence would hardly have appealed to him. To be sure, he feels the drag of futile chatter, as every eager spirit must: 'One must
grow accustomed in society to the fatigue of the
soul, as to the fatigue of the body in a campaign.'
But, nevertheless, light, gay, quick, easy conversation was a delight to him, not perhaps so much in the
form of scintillating cleverness as in the penetrating
interchange of mind with mind. His very voice had
the varied suggestion of instant sympathy which is
indicated in the charming phrase of the old Greek
novelist, 'The voice is the shadow of the soul.'
You felt that Fénelon's soul flowed about you, and
flowed into you, and mingled intimately with your
own.

For it is manifest that he was essentially social,
that he loved human beings as such, and would have
shared the view of the companionable lady who

said that she should like to talk for five minutes
with everybody in the world. It is true that even
he had his moments of revolt, moments when
solitude was alluring: 'I stroll, I find myself at
peace in the silence before God. Could there be
better company? With him one is never alone;
one is so often alone with men when one does not
want to listen to them.' But the revolt came rarely,
and in general he loved his friends, loved his family, loved to be with them and to care for them,
loved men and women at large, whoever they were.
Especially, he wanted to be loved, wanted to
charm and to attract human beings of all sorts,
'the desire to conquer hearts and to occupy them
with himself,' as Lemaître puts it, and as Saint-
Simon remarks a trifle more harshly: 'A coquettish
spirit, which wished to please everybody, from
the mightiest of the earth down to a workman and
a lacquey, and his gifts in this regard perfectly
seconded his desires.'

For there are people who go about the world
with a passionate desire to attract and only repel
by the excess of their ardor. Not so Fénelon:
He wanted to charm, and he succeeded fully.
From his earliest youthful days he gathered men
and women about him, and they clung to him to
the end, even in failure and disgrace. Here again
we have the masterly statement of Saint-Simon:
'A man who never tried to be cleverer than those
to whom he talked, who adapted himself to every
one without ever showing that he did so, who put

every one at his ease, and almost seemed to have the gift of enchanting, so that you could not quit him, nor resist him, nor fail to seek him again at the earliest opportunity.'

It may be said that to be a rich prelate makes such social successes comparatively easy. But Fénelon did not begin rich, and all his youth was an honorable struggle with narrow means. When money came, he used it and appreciated it. He kept up an ample establishment and a hospitality as wide-open as his heart. But he did not care for money to indulge himself. His tastes were simple, he ate little, and did nothing for mere display. No one better understood the insidious dangers of wealth and no one battled them more consistently. What he did like money for was to give, and he gave more and more widely as his means grew greater, gave to his own family, gave to the poor, gave to everyone who needed it, so that he died, ideally for one in his position, leaving neither a debt nor a fortune behind him.

It is evident that social response and success like Fénelon's necessarily meant a large and varied spiritual sensibility, and the sensibility extended, not only to social relations, but to all forms of art and beauty. The animosity which so many of the saints have felt against the arts is no doubt well founded: it is the nature of such things to tempt and seduce and betray. Fénelon knew it as well as anyone. But beauty was something which nerves like his could not altogether resist. He discusses paintings and statues with an almost caressing felicity, and he extends his exquisite tolerance even to the theater. Pascal could not condemn the theater bitterly enough. But the art of Racine and Molière touched Fénelon irresistibly, and if he found fault, it was rather from the artistic than the moral standpoint. And he loved nature almost as much as he loved humanity. He used to stroll alone in his park at Cambrai and forget the tumults and sorrows of the world with flowers and bird-song. All through his *Télémaque* the background of nature, without having the detail of modern description, has a sweet, large luminosity which suggests something of Greek models. But above all Fénelon loved the beauty of literature, in all its forms, Greek and other. He especially read and loved the classics, and liked to quote them freely when writing to correspondents who would understand. But he also admired the great writers of his own day and took very sensible ground in the hot controversy between the ancients and the moderns. He was even tolerant of that delicious vagabond La Fontaine and showed his appreciation of the *Fables* by writing similar fables of his own in prose.

For all his life he was an extraordinarily voluminous writer. His printed works fill ten solid octavo volumes, printed closely in double columns, and though the bulk of this is rather dreary theological controversy, there is also discussion of philosophy and politics, and much pure literature, fables and dialogues and pretty stories written for the benefit of his royal pupil and culminating in the *Télémaque*, a philosophical romance describing Telemachus's adventures in search of his father, with political and sociological arguments of a rather daring character for those days. The book was printed without Fénelon's consent, but it remained at least a school classic for two hundred years.

In all this vast work, even in the dullest theology, you feel Fénelon's peculiar charm. He knew how to say what he meant, to say it with directness, and ease, and grace, to make it strike home and stick. As one of his contemporaries put it, 'Do you not admire this man who has always the right term to express everything he thinks and who sees in everything just what is there?' Words, to Fénelon, were keen, sharp instruments that could be made to do his bidding. They were also delicate, fascinating toys, to play with in idle moments. At times they may have fooled him, but he had a gift at using them to conquer, to allure, and perhaps also occasionally to fool, other people. As a preacher he never seems to have been notable, but as a writer he stands among the very great. Just how much literary ambition he may have had, we do not know. He condemned ambition of all sorts, in the abstract. But assuredly to provide an educational classic that endures for two centuries is something of a literary achievement.

III

Yet any literary ambition that Fénelon may have cherished was quite obscured by hopes and struggles of a broader nature. He wanted above all things to direct, control, and manage men, to make the world over and make it better. He wanted to be a priest-statesman, like Richelieu and Mazarin, but with higher aims than theirs. Here again he vehemently disclaims all personal ambition. Yet he himself recognizes with acute and subtle discernment how difficult it is to separate the selfish from the unselfish: 'The air of a court,' he says, 'is pestilential: you breathe in ambition from it, as it were in spite of yourself.... There are a thousand pretexts for desiring fresh favors, and even when you do not directly desire them, you desire at least a good position and to be treated with respect. When you do not get these things, you suffer, and when you get them, you are too much preoccupied with them: the heart grows into them and is perverted by them.' Other observers saw the ambition in his case more clearly, and Saint-Simon, who was by no means unfriendly, speaks right out: 'He wanted to govern as a master who owes a reckoning to nobody, to rule in his own right without control.'

And it cannot be denied that Fénelon had peculiar gifts for such domination. The talent that made him a skillful spiritual director should have made him an able ruler of men. He understood them, he could persuade them, he made them willing to follow him. 'The great achievement of a superior man,' he says, 'is to give to each one his task, to set all the wheels in motion, to guide tranquilly the labor of many instruments.' He felt that he could do this, he did do it, as far as he had the opportunity, and he yearned to apply the gift in a far wider field. Always, of course, for the greater glory of God. Never for one moment did he admit to himself that he was seeking his own aggrandizement. If he wanted power, it was to use it, to make France the happiest, the noblest, the most God-fearing nation in the world, and to feel that he was the chosen instrument of divine Providence for bringing about this fortunate result.

All his life political speculation interested him, though it must be admitted that when, in early years, he tried direct, semipolitical action in converting the French Protestants, he did not altogether succeed. He was a radical in religion. He was a radical in politics, as those days went, at any rate his spirit would have been accepted as radical today, though his doctrines would not find favor in the twentieth century. He had not too much patience with Liberty, with a capital L, it was too apt to be confounded with license and excess: 'O my God! preserve me from that melancholy slavery which human insolence is not ashamed to call Liberty.' He was a decided royalist, believing that order should be solidly established. But then he held the startling creed that kings should exist for the benefit of their peoples, or should not exist at all. In one of the little Dialogues which he wrote for the Duke of Burgundy, Louis XI says to the historian De Commines, 'What! Should history not respect kings?' and De Commines replies: 'And should not kings respect history, and posterity, from whose censure they can by no means escape?' To Fénelon a king was a man, like other men, and needed to be advised and directed in the way he should go. Yet, as in everything, his tendencies to political radicalism were always tempered by a wise common sense, and when extremists proposed to blow up a naughty world, merely on the chance of improving it, he quietly replied: 'It is better to suffer for love of peace and order the evils inevitable under every sort of government, even the best ruled, than to shake off the yoke of all authority, giving way at once to the fury of the multitude, which acts without guidance and without law.'

Fénelon was not only a political thinker, he had excellent practical sense in attaching himself to the group which seemed likely to become the most influential in the kingdom. The two dukes Beauvillier and Chevreuse, with their duchesses, were very close to Madame de Maintenon, who was secretly married to King Louis, and through her they had access to the sovereign himself. Chevreuse was more of a reasoner, Beauvillier more of a doer, but both of them aimed at power, and they both were determined to use it for noble ends and to attain it by honorable means, if at all. Fénelon was on the most intimate terms with the dukes and with their wives, how intimate appears for example in his advice to Beauvillier as to his treatment of the Duke of Burgundy: 'You should not take a single step which should give any suspicion of eagerness; but you should keep as close to him as possible, with a simple, open, and affectionate manner, so as to induce him to give you his confidence.' With such prospects and such relations, it seemed as if a wide field of political usefulness was easily open to him.

But then there was Madame Guyon. Madame Guyon might be described as a spiritual adventuress, and she has left a picturesque account of her career in her lengthy autobiography. She belonged to an excellent family, was well brought up, married, and had five children. But such matters of this world interested her little. What she wanted was God and nothing else, to annihilate her earthly self and be lost in the vast, fluid abyss of the spirit, of which she daily and nightly dreamed. In other words, she had imbibed the doctrines of the Quietists, of whom Molinos was the chief representative, doctrines which had much affinity with the pantheism of the East and which were not in good repute in France because by rejecting all personal interest, even virtue and vice, they seemed seriously to threaten public morals. Madame Guyon's own natural tendency in the matter was accentuated by her romantic and much-criticized intimacy with a certain Père Lacombe, who carried enthusiasm to excess and finally died mad. Madame Guyon was not mad, or at least there was method in her madness, and she wrote various books which carried mystical ecstasy to a lofty, and to those who care for such things a most fascinating, pitch.

At any rate, she fascinated Archbishop Fénelon. They first met at the end of 1688 and Fénelon came at once under the spell. All his life he had been fighting the insinuating, engrossing, dominating self, seeking to get it down, to grind it down, to crush it out. Here was a woman who understood these things and could tell him the secret. The long correspondence between them is a human document of extraordinary psychological interest. There was no question of love in the lower sense, but all that the closest, tenderest spiritual affection, accentuated no doubt by the subtle difference of sex, could achieve was eminently developed. One passage of Madame Guyon's will suffice to show how close the relation was on her part, and though Fénelon was always more cautious, his tenderness seems to have been ardent enough: 'It is an intimacy that cannot be expressed, and short of being actually identical, nothing more intimate can be imagined. It was enough for me to think of him, to be more closely united to God, and when God held me most powerfully, it seemed to me that with the same arms with which he was holding me, he was holding him also.'

At first it seemed as if the connection with Madame Guyon might be a help to Fénelon politically. When she was introduced to Madame de Maintenon, the latter, with her natural keen responsiveness, was touched and felt the charm which Madame Guyon exerted over everyone. Madame de Maintenon allowed her new friend access to the girls' school at Saint-Cyr and seemed disposed to accept her influence. But the wind soon changed. Wise and cautious advisers warned of the danger to morals, Madame Guyon was politely got rid of, and even Fénelon, who at one time was considered as Madame de Maintenon's spiritual director, was quietly exchanged for someone of a more conventional order. No doubt the King was back of it all, and the King had never taken to Fénelon, even when he made him preceptor of the young prince. This Fénelon had a terrible way of speaking out to his lord and master: 'You do not willingly listen, Sire, except to those who flatter you with vain hopes. The persons whom you know to be the surest and most reliable are precisely those whom you dread and whom you avoid as much as possible.' This was a tone not commonly heard in the galleries of Versailles, and Louis felt, and made Madame de Maintenon feel, that the man who indulged in it had better be kept at arms' length, especially when he was inclined to an heretical woman who held mysterious doctrines that were convulsing the Church.

For the doubts and questions about Madame Guyon and her ideas culminated in the Quietist controversy which disturbed all France and set the closest friends at each other's throats. The basis of the quarrel seems too intangible to interest us much today. Fénelon, carrying out his own impulses, and much stimulted by Madame Guyon, asserted the doctrines of 'pure love' and 'passive prayer.' By pure love he meant that we should merge ourselves wholly in the love of God and should aim at loving Him without the least thought of present or future advantage to ourselves. By passive prayer he meant that we should not ask for particular blessings, but should lose and sink ourselves in a celestial contemplation in which all earthly matters, even the distinction of good and evil, are lost negatively in the pure love ecstasy.

It all seems very remote and far-away, and the thousands of pages written about it would be dreary enough, if it were not that human passion, the essence of all drama, was intimately involved and tangled up with it. The tumult spread beyond France, even to Rome, and not only priests and theologians, but men and women of the world, took sides and disputed desperately. And the whole human aspect of the conflict is summed up and personified in the two figures of Bossuet and Fénelon. Bossuet, Bishop of Meaux, was a great preacher, and a noble soul; Fénelon was, as we have seen, an enthusiast. And Bossuet dreaded enthusiasm, at any rate in its excesses. The tragedy of the conflict is emphasized by the fact that in early days they had been close friends, that Fénelon had looked up to Bossuet and learned from him, and that the older man had turned to his pupil with almost touching tenderness. But over Madame Guyon and her doctrines they split completely. Bossuet condemned her, Fénelon defended her. For four or five years the controversy dragged on, and when Fénelon was practically banished to his diocese of Cambrai, he appealed to Rome to have the final judgment of the Church upon the various writings in which he had set forth his cause with extraordinary energy and ingenuity. The Pope hated to interfere and was evidently bored by the whole business just as much as we are. But King Louis was so insistent that a decision had finally to be rendered — and it was against Fénelon, to the enduring triumph of Bossuet. Fénelon submitted, in appearance, accepted at once and implicitly the pronouncement of the Holy Father. But Bossuet felt, the whole world felt, that he was not in the least convinced; Madame Guyon had got too solid a hold upon him for that, and though they seldom met in later years, they corresponded and Fénelon clung to her to the end. What counts for us historically in the whole matter is the revelation of the human soul. Here were two of the noblest spirits who ever lived. They began by admiring and respecting each other. They ended by depreciating and abusing each other and by descending to mean and petty intrigue. Yet the curious thing is that through it all you love them both, each in his own way, and you feel that the best people you know, including yourself, might have done the same.

Fénelon was better able to bear his disappointment and his defeat by Bossuet, because his hopes and aspirations in the political field were left untouched. His earlier function as tutor of the Duke of Burgundy had enabled him to get a solid hold upon the spirit of that prince and even in his distant retreat at Cambrai and through all the agitation of theological disgrace that hold was hardly shaken, especially as it had the support of the two friendly dukes, who still retained their power over the King. The stories of the extraordinary transformation of the Duke of Burgundy's character under Fénelon's tuition are difficult to believe. He is said to have been born willful, violent, self-indulgent, impatient of all contradiction, and to have become docile, reasonable, industrious, and wise. At any rate, when Fénelon got through with him, he seems to have been a most promising candidate for future greatness and also to have retained a profound veneration for his teacher.

Then the Duke's father, the immediate heir to the throne, suddenly died, and at once the younger prince stood out as the center of all hopes and intrigues, almost necessarily bringing Fénelon into the highest prominence with him. The Archbishop of Cambrai became the most important man in France, and it looked as if all his eager plans for the good of the world might be fully realized. How large, how flexible, how modern, these plans truly were may be appreciated from his striking sentence: 'I love my family better than myself; I love my country better than my family; but I love the human race even better than my country.' Such a man might have done something to anticipate the League of Nations two centuries before its time.

Then there came another even more unexpected turn of Fortune's wheel. The Duke of Burgundy and his charming duchess, who was adored by both Madame de Maintenon and the King, died within a week of each other, in 1712, and for Fénelon the whole world went to pieces: there was simply nothing left. Perhaps the man never appeared more finely than in the dignity and serenity with which he bore the blow. A rare word or two shows his profound suffering: 'God has taken from us our hope for the Church and for the State. He formed this young prince; He adorned his spirit; He prepared him for greatest possible good; He showed him to the world — and all at once He destroyed him. I am filled with horror and am sick with the disaster, though with no visible sickness.' But outwardly he was tranquil and self-possessed and went about his daily functions untroubled, just as he had always done, giving no sign that the bottom had dropped out of his earthly life.

IV

And so it continued for the remaining years. He was still active, still useful, still immensely helpful to the many people who turned to him for comfort and support, for it is the highest tribute to his character that of all his friends and followers not one deserted him, even when his prospect of worldly power had slipped away. He even kept more or less in touch with the political world, advised the aged and broken King, and endeavored to form some connection with the Duke of Orleans, who was to become regent for the King's great-grandson after the King's death. But it was all rather hollow and meant little, and Fénelon realized that there was nothing left for him but God, and further, that God was enough and had always been the only solid reality in a world of fleeting and formless shadows.

Everywhere and at all times he knew that he had lived for God, however the hurry and tumult of the world may have disguised him. And the only thing that makes such living for God substantial, the profound emotional experience, had been his stay and comfort through all his struggles and all his difficulties. To be sure, his subtle and ingenious spirit had tended to cloud and chill simple emotion with elaborate theoretical speculation and theological argument. It was so easy and natural for his keen and fertile intellect to refine and split hairs, and when Bossuet or anybody else wanted to dispute and discuss, he was always ready and eager, and always delighted in a logical victory. The thousands of dusty pages that he left behind afford lamentable proof of it.

Yet beneath all the reasoning and theorizing there was always the depth of spirit, glowing and burning, making the dullest theory radiant and sublime. All his life Fénelon had battled with that hideous I, had sought to crush it, to overcome it, to merge it in the higher, vaster, divine infinity. Then came Madame Guyon, with her passionate visions of the final absorption of the soul in God: 'Such a soul sees only God everywhere, and all is God to it, not by reasoning, or even by vision or illumination, but by absolute identity and unity, which, making it God · by participation, destroys totally the vision of itself, and leaves nothing but God everywhere.' And under this influence Fénelon rose to heights of mystical rapture very nearly equivalent to Madame Guyon's own: 'In the nudity of pure faith one sees nothing, one desires to see nothing, one has no longer in one's self either thought or will; one finds everything in the universal unity, without dwelling upon anything distinct or particular; one possesses nothing, but one is possessed.' It may be pantheism, it may be meaningless, but it seems to have limitless depths of comfort and illumination for those who feel it.

Also, it must be recognized that all the time Fénelon had a fund of practical common sense with which his dear Madame Guyon was by no means so well supplied. When Bossuet aptly said of her that she 'prophesied the illusions of her heart,' Fénelon understood quite well what Bossuet meant. Fénelon warns his friend and cautions her, suggests his fear that 'sometimes you go too fast, that you mistake the sallies of your own vivacity for the promptings of God.' He himself was, after all, an agent, an instrument of the Church, and he was ready at all times to subordinate himself to the Church's good. After the Quietist struggle was over, he fought through the long conflict with the Jansenists, and this time on the orthodox side. And he said frankly that neither his own welfare nor Madame Guyon's should stand for a moment in the way of the Church's best interests: 'I would burn my friend with my own hands, and with joy would I burn myself, to save the Church.'

But what interests us most is the inner working of Fénelon's own spirit, and assuredly no keener, or subtler, or more penetrating analyst of such working ever lived. Take, for example, this effort to sound the depths of consciousness, together with the desolating sense of the futility of the effort: 'My state of mind cannot be explained, for I understand it less than anyone. As soon as I try to say anything of myself, for good or for evil, for trial or for consolation, I find it false even as I say it, because I have no consistency in any aspect whatsoever. I only see that the Cross repels me and that I cannot get along without it.' And here is another even more profound: 'I cling to things in a certain almost incredible fashion, but on the other hand, I regard them very little, for I am very easily detached from the greater number of things that might attract me. Yet all the time I feel a fundamental attachment to myself. After all, I cannot explain the basis of my soul: it escapes me, it seems to change from hour to hour. I can say nothing that the ensuing minute does not make appear to me false.' One seems to be reading a confession of Amiel.

To a spirit so fluid, so palpitating, so uncertain, and so disposed to probe itself, there came necessarily moments when even faith and hope seemed to slip away and vanish. To be sure, Fénelon was so solidly grounded in his beliefs that speculative question did not often disturb him. But though the groundwork of belief might be stable, the emotion, the exaltation, which gave belief all its real significance, was often elusive, often shadowy, often gave place to aridity, barrenness, and even sheer despair: 'Sometimes the spirit has to fast, like the body. I have no desire to write, nor to speak, nor even to have anybody speak of me, nor to reason or persuade anybody. I live from day to day, dryly, and with divers external annoyances that wear upon my soul.' Or take the following in which the veil is torn from the profoundest spiritual depths with a merciless clarity that has rarely been surpassed: 'For me, I am in a state of dry peace, obscure and languishing, without ennui, without pleasure, without thought of ever having any pleasure again, with no outlook for the future in this world, with a present insipid and often thorny, merely with something which carries me along, which softens all crosses, which keeps me contented though without any relish.... The world appears to me a poor comedy, which will disappear in a few hours. I despise myself even more than the world; I look at the worst side of everything; and it is at the very bottom of this worst side of everything here below that I find the shadow of peace.' It is easy to see how a confessor who thus confessed himself should have had sympathetic power to lead his penitents whither he willed.

And somehow I am all the time reminded of Matthew Arnold's description of Shelley, 'beautiful and ineffectual angel, beating in the void his luminous wings in vain.' Yet underneath the wing-beat in the cavernous void, underneath the flaunted, empty glory of the tragi-comic world, underneath even the broken ruin of one's self, there were always the everlasting arms, always the enduring, magnificent, solid, all-embracing unity of God, which was as real to Fénelon as it was to Francis or à Kempis. Get rid of your shallow, miserable, tormenting, encumbering self, reduce it to nothing, or to less than nothing: 'Become a real nothing in everything and everywhere. But you must not strive to add anything to this pure nothing. It is only nothing on which the world can get no hold. Nothing can lose nothing. Real nothing offers no resistance and it has no I to absorb it and destroy it.' Ineffectual wing-beats in the void? Perhaps. Yet, as Goethe said, 'to the materialist everything is God, to the pantheistic mystic, God is everything,' and there is a contrast universe-wide between the loss of everything in God and that complete loss of God in a tumult of multiplicity which Fénelon cries out against, and which forms the absorbing, dazzling, deafening, bewildering — and unsatisfying — whirlpool of the world today. For what is God but that something without which the human spirit can never be at rest?

THE GLORY OF SIN
BYRON

CHRONOLOGY

GEORGE GORDON BYRON.
   Born, London, January 22, 1788.
   At Harrow, 1801–1805.
   At Cambridge, 1805–1808.
   Hours of Idleness published 1807.
   Traveled in East, 1809–1811.
   Childe Harold published, March, 1812.
   Married Anna Isabella Milbanke, January 2, 1815.
   Wife left him, January 15, 1816.
   Left England, April, 1816.
   Left Italy for Greece, July, 1823.
   Died, Missolonghi, April 19, 1824.

LORD BYRON

VII

THE GLORY OF SIN
BYRON

I

IT MIGHT appear that a very small part of mankind has time to be interested in glory, the mass being simply absorbed by the quest for bread and butter with their various concomitants. But if the love of glory be translated to mean the desire to be known and praised and appreciated by many or few, the desire to escape from the maddening imprisonment of this perishable ego by more or less enduring affection and honor, then it may be said to be a rather widely and deeply inherent human instinct. And the love of glory in great rulers, great soldiers, great artists — and great saints — is merely the same instinct, developed and enriched and colored by the varied working of imagination, till it possesses and obsesses to the exclusion of almost everything else. You and I are sometimes astonished at the things we will do to win the regard and even the envy of our neighbors, and those with whom the effort for these things is the ruling passion will go to even more extraordinary lengths. Now it sometimes seems as if what used to be called sin was the cheapest and easiest method of obtaining a certain sort of glory. All men understand sin,

most men have a sneaking sympathy with it, or an
envy of it, at least in sexual forms. Even the saints
employ it to enhance the splendor of conversion, and
Augustine gets substantial profit out of what was
doubtless a very ordinary human career by turning
it into a gorgeous sexual revel to be laid before the
throne of God. Byron, at any rate, made luxuriant
use of sin, not only in a comparatively minor degree for itself, but still more for the satisfaction of
talking of it and flaunting it in resonant verses to
astonish and fascinate mankind.

George Gordon Byron was born in London,
January 22, 1788. He had a stormy inheritance on
both sides. His paternal ancestors drank, whored,
and spent money when they could get it, and his
father handsomely illustrated the tradition until he
died at thirty-six, in 1791. The mother was passionate, violent, erratic, and though she may have
loved her son, it was a wild way of loving. With the
son the love was less and the wildness was more.
The two most conspicuous elements in his early
life were his friction with his mother and the lame
foot which perhaps resulted from fault of hers at
his birth. He had the face of a god and the foot of a
cripple, and the dissonance haunted and tortured
his vanity all his life. After a childhood of poverty
and shifts, at ten years old he inherited the barony
and became sixth Lord Byron with the glorious
ancestral ruin of Newstead Abbey. It may have
been the sense of contrast that made him always
snobbishly insistent upon his rank and dignity as a

member of the English Peerage. His early education was as erratic as everything else about him,
but he read widely and waywardly and stored up a
vast treasure of words and facts in a singularly re-
tentive memory. In 1801 he went to Harrow, in
1805 to Cambridge. In neither place was he distinguished for learning, but he made many friends
and kept some of them. When he became independent, he plunged, both at London and at Newstead, into the rather vulgar dissipation which always had a certain charm for him, drank, whored,
and spent, as all the Byrons had done. But he had
a superb imagination which tortured and glorified
him. In 1807 he published his first book of poems,
and was laughed at, whereupon he wrote a fierce
satire, and laughed at the laughers, savagely. From
1809 till 1811 he traveled in the East and brought
back the first cantos of *Childe Harold*, which gave
him success so sudden and overwhelming that he
described it in his best-known sentence, 'I awoke
one morning and found myself famous.' For three
years he lived about town, which for him meant a
series of mad love-affairs, culminating in that with
his half-sister Augusta. In January, 1815, he married Miss Milbanke, probably as ill-suited to him as
a woman could be. A year later they parted in a
tempest of suspicion, reproach, and hatred. In 1816
Byron left England forever. He went first to Ge-
neva, then to Venice, where he reached the climax of
abandoned licentiousness. From this he was rescued
by his connection with the Countess Guiccioli, a

connection comparatively respectable by Italian standards. With her and with her family, and with Shelley, Hunt, and other English friends, he lived in Pisa and Genoa until 1823, when, finding that literature had given him all it could of glory and success, he went over to Greece, to assist in the liberation of that country. After a strenuous winter, during which he gave his means and his strength to the cause, and manifested remarkable energy, tact, common sense, and dignity under the most difficult circumstances, he died at Missolonghi on April 19, 1824.

The most striking fact in Byron's personality and character is the tremendous importance of his own ego and the brilliant and varied assertion which he was able to give to it. No doubt this same ego is the most important thing to all of us, but in many people it is more disguised and in most it is obscured instead of being so conspicuously flaunted by circumstances. Also, in persons of Byron's temperament, the ego, by reason of what present-day psychological slang calls the inferiority complex, or what for centuries has been known as self-conscious diffidence, becomes even more daring in the vehemence and persistence of its assertion. The assertion is established by the comments of all those who knew Byron intimately, as in the remark of Stendhal: 'Lord Byron was the unique object of his own attention.' It is shown clearly by his own sense of the tremendous position he occupied in the world: 'Hardly arrived at manhood, I had attained the zenith of fame.' And it is quite as manifest in the ironical persiflage which he showered upon those who were willing to swallow it, as when he said to a friend that 'he considered himself the greatest man existing,' and to the laughing exception of Napoleon replied, 'God, I don't know that I do except even him.' And precisely the same craving to substantiate the existence of that ravenous ego peers through more indirect observations: 'The great object of life is sensation — to feel that we exist, even though in pain.'

The shyness and self-consciousness of the oversensitive ego were of course most manifest in general society. Byron's rank, his accumulating glory, his extraordinary charm of personal appearance, and his abundance of talk when he felt inclined to it made him socially popular in London and everywhere else. But still he was shy in any large company, ill at ease, and always painfully aware of his crippled condition. What Trelawny says of one occasion seems to have been generally true, and Byron himself confesses it: 'On arriving, he was flushed, fussy, embarrassed, overceremonious, and ill at ease, evidently thinking a great deal of himself and very little of others.' With one companion he was much more comfortable, talking readily, gayly, and often with a most astonishing frankness and candor, saying everything he thought and a good many things he did not think, really.

Yet the social handicap made him at all times long for solitude and loneliness, though he might not enjoy them. He writes early from Newstead, 'There is such a sameness in mankind upon the whole, and they grow so much more disgusting every day, that, were it not for a portion of ambition, and a conviction that in times like the present we ought to perform our respective duties, I should live here all my life, in unvaried solitude.' When he was forced among men, the aversion sometimes reached the point of misanthropy, and he could be bitter, not to say savage, especially when his sensitive dignity felt that it had been affronted or injured. The outrageous insolence of his attacks upon Southey are merely typical of scores of others.

Yet he had friends, early and late, and he felt a singular tenderness for them even when they bored him, friends like Lord Clare, Matthews, Hobhouse, and Moore. It is interesting to compare two very different statements on this subject, that of Macaulay, whose temperament was certainly not Byronic, 'I have heard hundreds and thousands of people who never saw him rant about him; but I never heard a single expression of fondness for him fall from the lips of any of those who knew him well'; and that of Hobhouse, who was almost equally un-Byronic, but who felt the charm and speaks with far more authority: 'His power of attaching those about him to his person was such as no one I ever knew possessed. No human being could approach him without being sensible of this magnetic influence.'

So far as women were concerned, the charm has

never been disputed, and Byron attracted the most varying types, apparently without the slightest effort on his part. Back of all his contact with them there seems to have been a persistent contempt: 'I have always had a great contempt for women'; and some of those who knew him best denied his capacity for any ideal, self-forgetful affection. But women certainly absorbed him, from his early passion for his older cousin Mary Chaworth till the reign of Countess Guiccioli and his final departure for Greece. High or low made little difference. In the early days the absorption was largely that of vulgar dissipation. In the East it was promiscuous. In London later it was with ladies of social position, Lady Wedderburn, Lady Oxford, the mad Lady Caroline Lamb, and Mrs. Leigh. In Venice he recurred to more primitive types, fierce, passionate, disreputable creatures, who amused him, tormented him, and would not let him go till the Guiccioli drew him into a connection that for him was comparatively elevating. Everywhere and always it was women.

In London he tried to escape from the general horde by marrying. He did not love Miss Milbanke, he hated the thought of marriage anyway. It had always meant ruin in his family, as for that matter everything else had. But this girl was rich, she had position, she had good looks, she had brains, she was fond of him, why not try it? He tried it, but a year, in fact a day — and a night — was enough. Bell was high-minded, she was sensible, she was practical, but her practical sense irritated Byron to frenzy. Two touches in her own words suffice to show what she was. 'I never was nor ever can be so *mercilessly* virtuous,' she writes, 'as to admit *no* excuse for even the worst of errors.' And when she was asked if she feared personal violence from her husband, she replied, calmly, 'Oh, no, not in the least; my eye can always put down his!' It is easy to understand that Byron did not like an eye that would look down his. He teased her, bullied her, hated her, drove her off. There were a hundred good reasons for their separating, none of which, not even the incest, was definitely alleged, and probably there were times when they both regretted it. What is strange is that the only two women who should normally have influenced Byron were the only two who failed to do so, his mother and his wife. The faithful valet Fletcher said to Medwin that 'it was strange every woman should be able to manage his Lordship, but her Ladyship!' And Byron himself frequently acknowledged this susceptibility to influence. Mrs. Leigh, Lady Oxford, Caroline Lamb, Lady Melbourne, all swayed him for the moment as they pleased, and finally the Guiccioli took him in hand and did what she liked with him, on the whole for his good. He may have despised women, but they played a considerable part in his life.

Another element that shows Byron most characteristically is his dealings with money, which make a most curious tangle. In his youth he suffered the pinch of narrow means. When he later got cash into his hands, he spent in some respects lavishly, recklessly, piling up debts everywhere. There is evidence also that he was exceedingly and often quietly generous, extending his numerous benefactions freely. Yet there was an odd streak of meanness, side by side with the generosity. He sometimes promised and did not fulfill, he sometimes borrowed and forgot — conveniently — to repay. Also, with the curious perversity so characteristic of him, Byron liked to boast of his meanness. He proclaimed that money was the greatest power in the world: 'Money is the only true and constant friend a wise man puts his trust in.' In later years he took an impish pleasure in astonishing his friends by saving up gold sequins and ostentatiously counting them, and he told Hunt that 'at Harrow he would save up his money, not as other boys did, for the pleasure of some great purchase or jovial expense, but in order to look at it and count it.' Yet, when he went to Greece this would-be miser devoted a large part of his fortune to the public cause and all the evidence shows that he was not only liberal but eminently wise and judicious in the outlay of what he gave.

As regards intellectual life, Byron is laid open before us with as much clarity as in other matters. I have said that his education was wayward and erratic. So was his reading all his life, and his thinking also. He read vastly but superficially, and he loved to make display of what he read as in the amusingly pedantic notes to his poems. In philosophic matters, if the word may be associated with him at all, there was the same fitful petulance, nor was it any different with religion. Byron had none of Shelley's eager, penetrating, thoughtful investigation. He pricked, he dallied, he smiled, he shuddered, and passed on. There could be no more amusing comedy than the account of his dealing with the solemn Scotch Calvinistic doctor, Kennedy, who labored to convert him. Byron was polite, respectful, surprisingly quick in retort, even at moments touched; but he and the Christian spirit had little to do with each other. Yet he frequently proclaimed religious beliefs, whatever they might be, and above all he was superstitious, hated to begin any undertaking on a Friday, with all the other queer starts of such a temperament. And he certainly had plenty of the vague, inexplicable melancholy which sometimes leads to religion and sometimes results from it. He had moments, even days of mad, overstrained gayety, but the common-sensible wife gauged him accurately when she said, 'At *heart* you are the most melancholy of mankind, and often when apparently gayest.' And one thinks of Sainte-Beuve's remark about the melancholy 'natural to those who have abused the sources of life,' a remark curiously echoed by Byron himself: 'My passions were developed very early — so early, that few would believe me, if I were to state the period, and the facts which accompanied it. Perhaps this was one of the reasons which caused the anticipated melancholy of my thoughts — having anticipated life.'

The natural remedy for melancholy and too much thought of course is vehement action. Byron was well aware of this and longed for it: 'I prefer the talents of action...to all the speculations of those mere dreamers of another existence.' Yet by nature there was more of the dreamer than of the actor in him and the phrase, 'my evenings have that calm nothingness of languor, which I most delight in,' goes deeper than the other. He had no real zest for sports and his foot hampered him in them, though he was an energetic swimmer, rider, and boxer. There were moments when he thought eagerly of politics and war. He took his seat in the House of Lords, made some good speeches, and for the time seemed interested. All his life he proclaimed an ardent sympathy with revolutionary effort, and he shouted for liberty with thunderous resonance. But underneath the shouting lay a profound indifference and skepticism. After all, governments came back to men, and what were men? Kings and beggars they were all alike, and all contemptible: 'It is still more difficult to say which form of Government is the *worst* — all are so bad. As for democracy, it is the worst of the whole; for what is (*in fact*) democracy? an Aristocracy of Blackguards.' Yet here again, as with the money, Byron's conduct seems to belie his words. For when he plunged into the hopeless chaos of Greek affairs, he handled the complicated parties and issues with a tact

and patience and restraint that astonished everyone.

Yet, while in the Greek doings Byron's fundamental human sympathy is undeniable, it is perfectly clear that here also his ruling motive was the
desire for reputation, for glory, the passionate impulse to keep himself constantly in the public eye
and the public mind, in Lucretius's phrase, *volitare
per ora virorum*. Publicity, as a term, had not been
invented in Byron's day, but not even Sarah Bern-
hardt better understood the thing. To be sure, he
disclaimed it, as they all do. He cared nothing for
glory. 'There was a time,' he said to Lady Blessington, 'when fame appeared the most desirable of
all acquisitions to me; it was my "being's end and
aim," but now — how worthless does it appear!'
It may at moments have appeared worthless, but
it continued his being's end and aim to the very
last. As Lady Blessington herself puts it: 'The
end and aim of his life is to render himself celebrated.' Now, as I have already suggested, there is
one effective means of celebrity, or publicity, which
can be pretty surely counted upon, if you choose to
resort to it, and that is the glory of sin. To be sure,
sin, as a theory, seems to have somewhat faded
from the twentieth century, but the lurking shadow
of it in men's hearts still has a surprising power, and
it is easily called out. For souls like Byron's, souls
that delight in shocking the simple and puzzling the
wise, this form of glory has a strange attraction.
To be sure, some aspects of it did not appeal to

him. Glory through conquest and cruelty, like
Cæsar Borgia's, was out of his line. Nor, for all his
boasts of parsimony, would he have accumulated
money by crooked means, as Talleyrand did. His
form of temptation was sex, and sexual sin was a
gorgeous field for his imagination to expatiate in.
Yet even here there is a curious distinction. Byron
was not in the least like Casanova or Aaron Burr,
men who kept up a sexual revel for the endless
varied delight of it, without a moment of compunction or remorse. To Byron, the remorse was
the stamp of sin, without which the whole exhibi-
tion would have been worthless. Nor again was he
like Pepys, who sinned against his will and suffered
the pricks of conscience afterwards, real pricks. To
Byron the pricks were theoretical, like the sin, and
both made gorgeous material to flaunt before a
gasping world.

Thus there was always in his sinning the sense of
inchoate glory — in the adulteries of London, in the
sordid debaucheries of Venice. 'There was nothing
he thought more to his advantage than making you
stare at him,' says Leigh Hunt. Especially the
abnormal had a delicious shudder and must not be
missed. In this connection I am surprised at finding so little hint of homosexual perversions, which
one would think would have had a peculiar attraction. Various circumstances seem to suggest these,
but there is no definite charge to be based on either
Byron's own words or the researches of his biographers. It is obvious, however, that incest had a

peculiar, enthralling fascination. As to the actual tie with the half-sister Augusta Leigh, it would appear, after the publication of Lovelace's *Astarte* and the two volumes of *Correspondence* issued by Murray, that there could no longer be any question. Byron's own words to Augusta and to Lady Melbourne are unavoidably conclusive. But from the point of view of the glory of sin, the interesting thing is not so much the actual fact as Byron's perpetual references to something of the kind, the gloomy, shuddering, fascinated horror with which he constantly recurs to the fatal and irretrievable circumstance that had placed him forever among the damned. As he writes to Augusta of Francesca da Rimini, 'whose case fell a good deal short of *ours* — though sufficiently naughty,' and again, 'They say absence destroys weak passions — and confirms strong ones — Alas! *mine* for you is the union of all passions and of all affections.' And the comment of that flaccid creature Augusta herself is: 'It must be a dreadful idea that he *must* necessarily be wicked in *some* way.' Surely there is entire justice in the remark of Lady Blessington: 'Nothing seemed to please him more than being considered as a *mauvais sujet.*'

In all these intricate tangles one asks, How much did Byron consciously analyze himself? There are, especially in his journals, touches that occasionally go deep and with penetrating illumination. But in general one feels that his chief concern is with the impression he is producing on others. And everywhere and always one gets the sense of a petulant, spoiled boy, who has never grown up and is oppressed with a haunting desire to show off. Goethe indicated this especially with reference to Byron's thinking when he said, '*sobald er reflectirt, ist er ein Kind*,' as soon as he begins to reflect, he is a child. It is eminently true of the thinking, but it is true in other directions. There is the child's simplicity, the child's sheer outspokenness, not from candor but for effect, and it is the child explanation that best covers the strain of vulgarity which constantly crops out. This is not only evident in sexual doings, as in his habit of making everybody uncomfortable by his talk to women, even good women, as Leigh Hunt indicates. The vulgarity shows in money matters also. And there is an even deeper suggestion of it in his treatment of those whom he considered his inferiors, that is practically the whole world, not only his solicitor and his publisher, but even Hunt and Moore and Shelley. The essence of vulgarity is to trample on the feelings of others, and Byron did this with the expertness and the satisfaction of a rough English public school boy. Yet, on the other hand, when we are repelled by this lack of the finer touch in him, we must remember the impression of simple, boyish charm which he produced upon so many persons who met him. There is the hearty praise of Ticknor: 'After all, it is difficult for me to leave him, thinking either of his early follies or of his present eccentricities; for his manners are so gentle, and his whole character so natural and unaffected, that I have come from him with nothing but an indistinct, though lively impression of the goodness and vivacity of his disposition.' And it is well worth while to repeat the eulogy of Hobhouse, 'His power of attaching those about him to his person was such as no one I ever knew possessed. No human being could approach him without being sensible of this magnetic influence.'

II

Most of us, in asserting and disseminating the ego, however dominant, are confined within narrow limits. But when you have Byron's gift of words, you can fling yourself far out over the universe and make it listen. And Byron used this gift of expression to the full. To be sure, he by no means always acknowledged publicity as a motive: 'To withdraw *myself* from *myself* (oh, that cursed selfishness!) has ever been my sole, my entire, my sincere motive in scribbling at all.' Or, he insists that he writes for the refuge and relief of it: 'If it were not for some such occupation to dispel reflection during *inaction*, I verily believe I should very often go mad.' Yet he said of himself that he could never keep a secret, and it is quite obvious that his writing was merely a means of telling all his boy's secrets to the whole world and making that world know him and remember him.

The methods of Byron's writing were as characteristic as the purpose of it. He liked to theorize about literature. The elaborate controversy with Bowles as to the merits of Pope is a sample of what Byron was worth critically. He wrote with splendid vigor, but his thinking, as Goethe said, was always that of a child. And his own work, as he frankly confessed, was far removed from the classical standards he admired. He wrote under the impulse of the moment, dashed off the best of it with little correction, though undoubtedly it had been working in his head long before. And the product had the defects of the method. It was hasty, diffuse, ill-arranged; but also it had the fire, the vigor, the large and splendid sweep which are the privilege of inspiration at its best.

These qualities show in all the long list, from *Childe Harold* to *Don Juan*. Sometimes the weakness prevails, sometimes the strength, but both, and the stamp of improvisation, are always there. It may safely be said that *Don Juan* sums up and epitomizes the whole in strong points and weak points both. When Byron came to it, he had fully developed the process of release by which every great artist rids himself of the trammels and traditions which the example of his predecessor has fastened upon him. Through Italian influence he had hit upon the *ottava rima*, which had been little used in English before and which was so admirably adapted to the peculiarities of his genius. Under his flying thoughts and fingers the subtle, supple octave, with endless surprises of rhyme and rhythm, develops all its wealth of grace, of energy, of satire, of pathos, of varied color, of shifting ascent and descent. It fits life, and above all it fits Byron like a glove.

For it need hardly be said that self-portrayal is the essence of all this long and varied list of achievements. Byron touched pretty much everything in heaven and earth, but he touched it all from the point of view of its appeal to him and his response to it. The same self-portrayal is of course obvious in his prose. There are persons who find his letters among the best ever written. To me they seem far inferior to those of Lamb or Keats or Cowper, not to speak of Voltaire or Flaubert. But they undeniably have significant touches of self-revelation and the journals have many more. Yet I hardly regret the memoirs, the destruction of which caused such far-reaching controversy. It does not appear that Byron really spoke out in them: they seem to have been ugly rather than profound. But the huge sequence of the poems is nothing more nor less than a continuous autobiography. It was in vain for Byron to deny his identity with his heroes. Their superficial wanderings and adventures were obviously invented. Their inner nature was that of their creator and every word and gesture was significant of him. Especially is this true of *Don Juan*. Juan himself of course is a freakish, fantastical figure, though still with many hints of his source. But in page after page all pretense at the objective is thrown aside and the poet tells his own story with a freedom, an ease, a crowding wrath, or tenderness, or mockery, far more varied and penetrating than Augustine's or Rousseau's. He turned his own soul into one of the three great narrative poems of the English language.

Everywhere in this fiery record there is the portrayal of self in the workings of ambition, the fierce effort and desire to be at the top.

> Well, if I don't succeed, I *have* succeeded,
>   And that's enough. . . . .
> . . . . I've paid, in truth,
> Of late the penalty of such success,
> But have not learn'd to wish it any less.

And at the same time there is the bitter recognition of the equal futility of success and failure:

> We wither from our youth, we gasp away —
> Sick — sick; unfound the boon — unslaked the thirst.
> . . . .
>
> Love, fame, ambition, avarice — 'tis the same,
> Each idle, and all ill, and none the worst.

There is the feverish, mad rush of action, action of any sort as a refuge from the tormenting inefficacy of thought.

> But quiet to quick bosoms is a hell.

And all the nerve-driven heroes, Ezzelin, Conrad, Lara, Manfred, Cain, surge through their thrilling tempests of adventure, or at least long for them, precisely as Byron himself did. And on the one hand there is the constant recognition that the mad acting leads nowhere and accomplishes nothing.

On the other there is the desperate effort to find a lofty heroism in the tumult of the destruction itself:

> Seek out — less often sought than found —
> A soldier's grave, for thee the best;
> Then look around, and choose thy ground,
> And take thy rest.

Needless to say that there is love everywhere, love in all its aspects, unless perhaps that of serene and tranquil attachment. There is the despair of passion:

> When we two parted
> In silence and tears,
> Half broken-hearted
> To sever for years,
> Pale grew thy cheek and cold,
> Colder thy kiss;
> Truly that hour foretold
> Sorrow to this.

There is the darker despair of disillusion and regret:

> No more — no more — Oh, never more on me
> The freshness of the heart can fall like dew.

And again the autobiographical dissection goes widely into more varied human relations. There is the love of solitude and the insistence upon its unfailing charm, as against the noise and dust and hollowness of society:

> But in Man's dwellings he became a thing
> Restless and worn, and stern and wearisome,
> Droop'd as a wild-born falcon with clipt wing,
> To whom the boundless air alone were home.

BYRON

Yet there was constant sojourn in man's dwellings, just the same, and keen observation and criticism of them, and there was a close, sincere, clinging tenderness, and when it came to the Southeys and the Castlereaghs and a hundred others, there was wild ferocity of hate, which is sometimes detestable and sometimes ignoble, but nearly always magnificently picturesque.

Naturally Byron's reflection, both the acute and the shallow, poured itself with a rush into his poetry, reflection on the cause and the end of things, on God and Man. Everywhere there is a tumult of showy, casual speculation on kings and beggars, on statesmen and prelates, on authors and charlatans, and on himself. There is religion, sometimes in shuddering or comforting hints of the fierce Calvinism in which he had been brought up, which makes one think of that jovial old Calvinist, Lyman Beecher, who loved Byron and was confident that if he could talk to him for an hour, he could make him see the light. But more often the religion is that vague, naturalistic pantheism, which Byron perhaps imbibed from Rousseau and Wordsworth, but to which he gave a passionate personal touch that was all his own:

> I live not in myself, but I become
> Portion of that around me; and to me
> High mountains are a feeling...
>
> .   .   .   .
>
> Are not the mountains, waves, and skies, a part
> Of me and of my soul, as I of them?

And behind even the pantheism is the vague longing, the vast desire, for something, somewhere something higher, nobler, at any rate something different, the desire which no god can explain and no heaven can satisfy. It is this longing which Matthew Arnold refers to, in his admirable lectures on Celtic literature, where he differentiates the Celtic strain from the Germanic and speaks of 'all Byron's heroes, not so much in collision with outward things, as breaking on some rock of revolt and misery in the depths of their own nature':

> The fire that on my bosom preys
> Is lone as some volcanic isle;
> No torch is kindled at its blaze —
> A funeral pile.

And again:

> Count o'er the joys thine hours have seen,
> Count o'er thy days from anguish free,
> And know, whatever thou hast been,
> 'Tis something better not to be.

Then, in the midst of the gloom, come the sparks and flashes of Satanic laughter. It is said that in private life Byron could be merry and gleeful, but the laughter in his verses is for the most part harsh, dreary, and bitter. M. Maurois compares him on this side as on others with Shakespeare, but Byron never, never, caught Shakespeare's irresistible, enveloping sunshine. To Shakespeare the world is mysterious. It might have been different, it might have been better. But as it is it is vastly curious and delightful. To Byron the world is ridiculous and the world and Byron and God might have been different and better and ought to have been, but how? Yet Byron's laughter has its splendor, all the same. It is often ugly, it is oftener vulgar, as in the savage sketch of Lady Byron as Donna Inez in the first canto of *Juan*,

> Her memory was a mine: she knew by heart
>   All Calderon and greater part of Lopé,
> So that if any actor miss'd his part
>   She could have served him for the prompter's copy.

But in its glittering, compelling surge it sweeps away pain and pleasure and love and hate and life and death and the reader and the laugher himself:

> And if I laugh at any mortal thing,
>   'Tis that I may not weep; and if I weep,
> 'Tis that our nature cannot always bring
>   Itself to apathy.

And so heaven and hell alike are mixed and lost in the preposterous turmoil.

It is not to be supposed that, with Byron's poetry so vividly reflecting his soul, the love of glory and especially the resounding glory of sin would fail to find a place in it. At every step he seems to be saying 'You see me here, me, the great Byron. You wonder at me, you adore me. But you really do not know how bad I am. I hardly know myself, and when I realize it, it amazes me, it horrifies me, it delights me.' This outcry in

Byron is by no means Emerson's gently ironic ex-
clamation, when his critics said that the impulses
he professed to follow might be from below, not
from above: 'They do not seem to me to be such;
but if I am the Devil's child, I will live then from
the Devil.' In Byron it was furious and not ironic
at all. He was determined to be the Devil's child,
he was proud of it, and he wanted everybody to
know it, not only the Devil's other children, but
still more the Bell Milbankes, who believed themselves to be the children of God.

Hence the incessant flaunting bravado of all
sorts of cultivated or intimated crimes and pec-
cadilloes. There is the bravado of miserliness, the
counting and the stinting of his money,

> So for a good old-gentlemanly vice,
> I think I must take up with avarice.

There is the bravado of irreligion, and when you
were not shuddering at divine possibilities, you
could mock at them. You could mock at priests
and churches and ceremonies and all the other
nonsense, and you could set your dark-browed
rebel heroes, your Conrads and Laras and Man-
freds and Cains, to turning the world upside down
with sacrilegious ribaldry.

Best of all was the inexhaustible bravado of sex.
All those English were sinning in dark corners
and covering it up with conventional morality as
dusty and hollow as the grave. You could drag
their sins out into the sunlight, and pile your own

graver sins on top of them, and dance around the whole with an endless flare of ghoulish mockery. There was that story of incest. Whether it was true or not, they were all believing it in England. What could give more zest to life than to make Manfred love his sister, and Cain love his sister, and to be perpetually tossing to and fro wild hints of things that had to shun the light of day:

Too brief for our passion — too long for our peace —
Was that hour — can its hope — can its memory cease?
We repent — we abjure — we will break from our chain —
We must part — we must fly — to unite it again.

So it comes back always to the wayward, mischievous, malignant child. It may be true, as Moore says, that he sometimes shrank from seeing himself as the world saw him: 'Like a child in a mask before a looking-glass, the dark semblance which he had, half in sport, put on, when reflected back upon him from the mirror of public opinion, shocked even himself.' But the instinct was too strong and the pleasure too great to be ever foregone. He was like a schoolboy, shunned and admired by his companions for his misdeeds, one who walks apart, gloomy, scowling, biting his finger-nails, as Byron did, but secretly — and sourly — delighting in the distinction and superiority of wickedness. *Sobald er reflectirt, ist er ein Kind*, said Goethe. But all his life he was a child, a hateful child, a lovable child, but always a child who was gorgeous and magnificent.

III

If, then, the egotism of Byron's life and Byron's poetry is so absorbing so engrossing, it will naturally be asked why he should have swept away millions in his time and should continue to have such a solid hold upon the world a hundred years later. The answer is, first, that he had the poet's divine gift of making even his egotism beautiful, and, second, and even more important, that in expressing his own ego he was doing the same kind office, at any rate in many aspects, for the ego of all of us; and to all of us, as to him, however we may conceal it or disguise it, our own ego is the thing that counts. The whole universe is nothing but you or I. We know it and keep still about it, sometimes. Byron knew, it and said it right out, with a breadth and splendor that are eminently gratifying to you and me as they were to him. As his best biographer, Miss Mayne, puts it, what draws us and holds us to him is 'his enthralling humanity.'

As to love, it may be said that Byron did not portray its serene and enduring security, if such a thing exists, because he did not know it. He at least seized its restless, feverish, devouring aspects, as well as its consuming sweetness. For the sweetness there is the glittering, sparkling, mocking climax in *Don Juan*, which piles up all the enchantments of the world to end in

> But sweeter still than this, than these, than all,
> Is first and passionate love — it stands alone,
> Like Adam's recollection of his fall.

BYRON

For the fever and disillusion there is the cry of Harold:

> Who loves, raves — 'tis youth's frenzy; but the cure
> Is bitterer still.

And mankind, or womankind, will not soon forget the brief and poignant statement of a universal truth,

> Man's love is of man's life a thing apart,
> 'Tis woman's whole existence.

Again, the larger world of human relations in general has seldom been painted with more power and vigor than in *Juan* and *Beppo*. The higher and the nobler may not always be there, but common passions and pursuits and interests, as we know them in others, and in ourselves, are touched with a vividness quite unsurpassed:

> Without, or with, offence to friends or foes,
> I sketch your world exactly as it goes.

And the sense of isolation that overwhelms us in the midst of hurrying, bustling, indifferent crowds, the loss of our identity, of our existence even, in that mad tumult, has it ever been caught better than by one who had felt it to the very bottom of his soul?

> But 'midst the crowd, the hum, the shock of men,
> To hear, to see, to feel, and to possess,
> And roam along, the world's tired denizen,
> With none who bless us, none whom we can bless;
> Minions of splendour shrinking from distress!

None that, with kindred consciousness endued,
If we were not would seem to smile the less,
Of all that flatter'd, follow'd, sought, and sued;
This is to be alone; this, this is solitude!

Nor has anyone better expressed for us all the splendor of swift, vigorous action, action that sweeps us out of ourselves and for the moment at any rate makes us know we are alive. The action of Byron's heroes may not be always lofty, may be almost never unselfish; it is at least full of absorbing, oblivious variety and power. The stormy adventures of Conrad and Lara, the unexampled fury of Mazeppa's ride, make every nerve and fiber in us tremble and quiver with exultant, sympathetic effort. Probably no battle piece in the world is better known than the description of Waterloo in *Childe Harold*, and it must be admitted that Byron's feeling and portrayal of the futility and the obscene horror of war is fully equal to his sense of its glory. While the quick energy of rhythm, as at once interpreting and stimulating action, has never been better illustrated than in the fiery rush of *Sennacherib*:

The Assyrian came down like a wolf on the fold,
And his cohorts were gleaming in purple and gold;
And the sheen of their spears was like stars on the sea,
When the blue wave rolls nightly on deep Galilee.

Nor are the elements of heroism and self-sacrifice by any means wholly lacking in Byron's mad tumult of adventure. His enthusiasm for Italy and Greece and for liberty everywhere must be set down as not all rhetoric, since he gave his life for them in the end. And the pulse will leap and the nerves will thrill at an outcry like this:

> For I will teach, if possible, the stones
> To rise against earth's tyrants. Never let it
> Be said that we still truckle unto thrones; —
> But ye, our children's children! think how we
> Show'd *what things were* before the world was free!

And are there many of us who, through all the tumult and all the passion, and even all the sacrifice, do not feel the need and the relief of the vagrant diversity of laughter, even when the laughter is quaint and impish as Byron's? No matter how vastly serious we are, there are moments when the futility of our own efforts, and especially of other people's, overcomes us, and we enter freely and delightedly into Byron's mocking mood. The mad child laughs at glory, laughs at effort, laughs at wisdom, laughs at virtue, and especially at all the pinchbeck simulations of virtue, and we can but laugh with him, even while we weep.

And if Byron is a child when he reflects, are there many of us, even the great Goethe himself, who are much more, when we are thrown flat against the insoluble problems of life and death? Do we not drift vaguely and uncertainly through the shadowy realms of speculation, now shivering and shuddering at pain and grief and nonentity, as Byron did, now flinging rebellious defiance in the eternal question, which has always been asked and which has never yet been answered, the question why an omnipotent good God should make his creatures to be miserable? In these latter world-shaken days are not the theorizings of modern science and the dreamings of ancient and modern philosophy and even the polysyllabic self-assurance of modern psychology admirably summed up in the resonant rhetoric of Byron's stanza?

> Between two worlds life hovers like a star,
>   'Twixt night and morn, upon the horizon's verge.
> How little do we know that which we are!
>   How less what we may be! The eternal surge
> Of time and tide rolls on, and bears afar
>   Our bubbles; as the old burst, new emerge,
> Lash'd from the foam of ages; while the graves
>   Of empires heave but like some passing waves.

Also, are there not some of us, many of us, who, like Byron, seek refuge from the arid waste of thought in the intimate solitude, the peopled loneliness, of nature? When you walk in these autumn woods, with the rich colors of death about you, with the ceaseless murmur of the insects and the warble of the bluebirds and the slow drift of the October clouds before the soft south wind, do you not instinctively recall the words of Byron?

> There is a pleasure in the pathless woods,
> There is a rapture in the lonely shore,
> There is society where none intrudes,
> By the deep Sea, and music in its roar:
> I love not Man the less, but Nature more,
> From these our interviews, in which I steal
> From all I may be or have been before,

BYRON

To mingle with the Universe, and feel
What I can ne'er express, yet cannot all conceal.

Even when it comes to Byron's zest for the glory of sin, is there not something in us somewhere that responds? Underneath all our well-worn garb of smug, conventional morality, have we not lurking in a dark corner some sin that we should commit if we dared? When Byron dares and does that which he feels he was made to do, is there not something in us that echoes while it condemns? Since even the good Emerson could say, 'If I am the Devil's child, I will live from the Devil.'

Yet through all the tangle of the glory of sin and the sin of glory and the achievement of glory that has endured for a century and may endure for many centuries, perhaps Byron nowhere appears better than in his delight over the Italian epitaphs which he stumbled upon in the Certosa cemetery at Bologna: 'I found, too, such a pretty epitaph in the Certosa cemetery, or rather two: one was

Martini Luigi
Implora pace;

the other,

Lucrezia Picini
Implora eterna quiete.

That was all; but it appears to me that these two and three words comprise and compress all that can be said on the subject.... They have had enough of life — they want nothing but rest — they im-

253

plore it, and *eterna quiete....* Pray, if I am shovelled into the Lido churchyard in your time, let me have the *implora pace*, and nothing else, for my epitaph.' And what better in the whole wide universe could he implore?

THE END

INDEX

INDEX

INDEX

INDEX

Dumas, Alexandre, 87, 94, 106

Elias, Brother, 65, 66
Elizabethan drama, 35, 36
Emerson, Ralph Waldo, 246, 253
d'Enghien, Duc, 175

Farnese, Julia, 20
Fénelon, François, 66, 145; chronology of his life, 186; a born saint, 187; summary of his career, 187, 188; as a director of souls, 188–96; pen-portrait of, 197; his intelligence, 197, 198; was a born aristocrat, 198, 199; his conversational powers, 199; was social in his nature, 199–201; his use of money, 201; his appreciation of art, 201, 202; his *Télémaque*, 202, 203; as a writer, 202, 203; wished to be a priest-statesman, 204; as a political thinker, 205, 206; his practical sense in politics, 206, 207; and Madame Guyon, 207–11; and the Duke of Burgundy, 212, 213 (cf. 188, 206, 207); lived for God, 214, 215, 218, 219; as self-analyst, 216–18
Fouché, Joseph, 174, 180
Fox, Charles James, 178
France, Anatole, quoted, 6, 20, 37
Francis of Assisi, Saint, chronology of his life, 40; summary of his career, 41, 42; the first principle of his religion (poverty), 42–48, 120; the second principle of his religion (obedience), 48–53; would eschew pride of intellect and secure abasement of the will, 51, 52; the third principle of his religion (chastity), 53–55; part

played by women in his life, 55; his subdual of lower instincts, 55, 56; his abuse of the body, 56; his experience with the lepers, 57; richness and depth of his inner spiritual life, 58, 59; was a man of action, 59; chooses life of preaching rather than life of prayer, 60; his self-glory, 61–63; his gift of speech, 63, 64; his practice of organization, 64, 65; his Order, 64, 65; his contact with individual souls, 66, 67; his impulse of wandering, 67–73; is permeated with God, 71–73
Francis of Sales, Saint, 66, 145, 189, 195

Gandia, Duke of, brother of Cæsar Borgia, 4, 22, 23, 30
Glory, love of, 223, 234, 235
God, 136–42, 144, 146, 180–83, 214, 215, 218, 219
Goethe, Johann Wolfgang von, 85, 218, 237, 239, 247, 251
Golden Rose, 29, 30
Goncourt, 108
Grand (*née* Worlée), Madame, 153
Gregorovius, 23
Gregory IX, Pope, 50
Grey, Earl, 166
Groot, Gerard, 114
Guède, M., 102
Guérin, Eugénie de, 109
Guiccioli, Countess, 225, 229, 230
Guyon, Madame, 137, 141, 188–90, 199, 207–11, 215, 216

Hamilton, Alexander, 178
Hammerken, Gertrude, mother of Thomas à Kempis, 113

259

INDEX

INDEX

INDEX

darkness,' 149; summary of his career, 149, 150, 166; neglected by family, 150, 151; his *Mémoires*, 151, 161, 179; his mother, 151; his artificial stolidity, 152; his relation to women, 152–54, 179; his friendships with men, 154, 155; his attitude toward money, 156–61; his delight in society, 161–64; his attitude toward books, 162, 163; as regards his æsthetic interests, 163, 164; his appearance and manner, 164; his conversation, 165; his social charm, 165, 166; his industry and power of labor, 166, 167; physical weaknesses and peculiarity of, 167 (cf. 150); his political ideas and action, 167–72; was a power for peace, 169, 170; and Napoleon, 170, 171, 173–76; never manifested gift of leadership, 172; his observation of mankind, 177, 178; lacking in self-analysis, 179, 180; and God and the Church, 180–83

Thomas à Kempis, chronology of his life, 112; summary of his career, 113, 114; the *Imitation*, 114, 117, 119, 121–24, 129–31, 133, 135, 140, 142–46; on subdual of self in wants and desires, 120–28; on self, 120–22, 128; on riches, 122; on love of reputation, 123; on pursuit of knowledge, 124, 125; on the arts, 125; on the outdoor world, 126; on the temporal and the eternal, 127; on subdual of self in reference to others, 128–36; on habit of solitude, 128–30; on desire to rule, 130; on anger, 130, 131; on aversion, 131; on curiosity, 132; on silence, 133; on friendship and affection, 133, 134; relation to family and relatives, 134; on love for woman, 135; on obedience, 135; on humility, 135, 136; on subdual of self with regard to God, 136–42, 144, 146

Thomas of Celano, quoted, 63
Ticknor, George, 237
Tolstoy, Leo, 43
Tombs, sculptural, 32
Trelawny, Edward John, 227
Twentieth century, characteristics of, 43, 48, 53, 54, 87, 129, 135, 169, 192, 234

d'Urfé, Marquise, 99

Vitrolles, Baron de, and Talleyrand, 156, 157
Voltaire, François Arouet de, 78, 87, 91, 182

Waldstein, Count, 104
Walpole, Horace, 91
Wanting, abolition of, 43, 120
Wedderburn, Lady, 229
Wellington, Duke of, 171
Will, abasement of, 52
Wordsworth, William, 243

X Y Z papers, 159